Vanessa,

For the Lost Sheep!

Jerry

2011 is all about new
beginnings for you!

"In "83 Lost Sheep" Gerry Stoltzfoos calls the church to face the reality of the lostness of our nation. 83 out of 100 people don't go to church anywhere! Gerry uses Luke 10 as a blow by blow description of what we've done wrong, and how we can begin to do church planting right. In addition to great content, Gerry's heart for church planting is infectious and shines through in this book. Quite honestly, Gerry breaks the mold of what kind of churches can plant churches. Talk about a guy who is living what he's preaching. Gerry Stoltzfoos is a planter of church planters, and I'm privileged to work with him."

- Matt Keller; pastor of Next Level Church, Ft. Myers, FL; founder of Next Level Coaching & author of *The Up the Middle Church* (www.MyNextLevel.me)

"I have to be honest: while reading the first three chapters I didn't believe in the premise of the book. The concept that planting churches is the answer to reaching lost people seemed a bit off to me. But by the end of the book, my stance changed greatly. Is planting churches the answer? If done in the way that Gerry outlined in this book, then I believe it could be."

- Ryan Dagen, Youth Pastor, Gap Community Church, Gap, Pennsylvania

There are some basic assumptions holding back the church in America. This book blows some of those assumptions out of the water and clears the way for leaders to see things the way Jesus shows them to us! "83 Lost Sheep" ought to be required reading for every church leader and ministry student in the country.

- Jason Fitch, Lead Pastor, Freedom Valley Church, Tulsa, OK.

"Gerry and I share a common history among the Amish Mennonite community in Lancaster County, PA. I walked with Gerry and Julie as a friend through many of the stories in this book. Reading it made me laugh and cry as I reflected on how faithful God is. Gerry gives the straight story on his journey in church planting, pulling no punches. The book is a great encouragement to anyone wanting to plant a church or living in the trenches of ministry."

- Omar Beiler, Eurasia Regional Director, Assemblies of God World Missions

"Gerry, the content made me laugh, and then cry, but it also gave me a lot to consider regarding church planting. I'm proud of you as a friend and am excited about what God is helping you to accomplish for the kingdom of God. To Him be the glory, and thanks to you for being faithful to the call."

- Merrill Smucker, Lead Pastor, Gap Community Church, Gap, Pennsylvania

"This book will inspire you to take a fresh look at the words of Jesus and refocus your life on the reason that He came! You'll discover that you can make a big difference in reaching the 83 lost sheep!"

-Sam Masteller, Lead Pastor, Freedom Life Christian Center, Christiana, Pennsylvania

83 LOST SHEEP

Reaching A Nation That Has Given Up On Church

DEDICATION

It was May 1, 1992. I backed the big, borrowed, moving truck up to the side door of the home God had provided for my wife Julie, our five-year old Candace, three-year old Shawna, and one-year old Evan. As we unloaded, Candace froze in her tracks, a brand new consideration entering her brain and clogging up every thought she had in the first five years of her life.

"Dad," she asked urgently, "will I ever get to see my friends again?"

Her question ripped through my soul like a baseball bat through a watermelon, splattering crazy thoughts and sticky emotions everywhere. I had just risked every solid thing in my entire life to move my family far away from the best grandparents they could ever wish for, the warmth of a precious church family, and everything they had known. I did not have an income, life was very uncertain, and I had never planted a church before. Suddenly, the cost of the decisions I had made became very unpleasant.

"Of course you will Candace," I heard myself say to her with less confidence than I wanted to convey. "We'll make sure of it."

And then I wondered: How would we do that?

Candace ran off to play, satisfied that if her Daddy said it, it would happen. I, however, did not feel anywhere near her level of confidence about her Daddy's words, and wondered to myself when he would learn to make less rash promises!

As I worked, Julie appeared around the corner of the house, smiling as she came. I told her about Candace's question, and our eyes locked for a minute as we contemplated the challenges we were up against. Then I saw Julie square her shoulders and say these incredible words:

"Let's get the kids together and ask God for new friends, here!"

That's what we did, and God answered that prayer within 48 hours. My soul crisis was averted.

This church and this vision, ridiculous by any reasonable standard, could never have happened without the visionary, faith-filled, beautiful woman I am married to. My covenant with her is more important than the vision, and my commitment to those three kids, and their younger brother Luke (born a year later), is far deeper. They patiently taught me, coached me, and encouraged me as only those who know you deeply can.

Julie's faith challenges me, inspires my courage, and makes me fall in love with her all over again. Her beauty captured my eyes the first time I saw her and does so even more now, 30 years later. But it is her faith in moments like these that create the exciting life we get to live.

I dedicate this book to Julie.

CONTENTS

Introduction: One Sad Day

Fact: 83 out of 100 people living in the northeastern United States don't know Jesus.[1]

So few pastors are aware of this statistic – even my friends who are aggressively reaching out to their communities haven't heard this.

I remember sitting with Omar Beiler and Merrill Smucker, two friends and colleagues of mine, sometime in 1986. It was an informal staff meeting, and we sat together as we often did at a local diner, having breakfast and drinking coffee. In those days I remember someone telling me that church attendance in the United States was approaching 50%-60%. Whether they were right or not, I'm not sure, but this became our topic of conversation that morning.

"What an exciting time for the church in America," Omar said from across the table. "Attendance is rising and we're seeing a resurgence of godliness in our country."

The church's momentum was so strong in the mid-1980s that I remember Jimmy Swaggert looking into a television camera, pointing his finger, and telling a member of Congress that the way he was voting was wrong.

And the congressman changed his vote.

But just when the church seemed to be at its strongest point, scandals sent a shivering crack through the structure.

In 1987 the Jim Bakker story broke.

A year after that the Jimmy Swaggert story came out.

These two men were two of the loudest voices for God in those days: one religious and stridently pious; the other warm and down-to-earth. Their respective falls rocked the church world. Their reported hypocrisy and deception validated the skeptics in our society.

One Christian leader stated that those two scandals set the Christian Church back ten years.

"That guy is wrong," Omar said. "It will be 25 to 50 years before we can get back the momentum we had in this country before those two fell."

Here we are, 23 years later, and we're still hitting new lows in church attendance.

I started experimenting in ministry in 1983 when I was a volunteer intern at my local church, Victory Chapel. 26 years later I first discovered that church attendance had dropped from its heady level of near 50% in the late 1980s to 17%.

A 33% drop. And it happened while I was on watch.

I can't live with that.

I feel like we've lost. My fellow pastors and I should be weeping in shame, but we're not shedding a tear.

Instead it seems like we are often fighting over the remaining 17%.

That was my saddest day, when I realized that my generation of pastors lost over 30% of the US population. I had no idea it had gotten that bad. I realized that my goal of starting 100 churches in twenty years was not going to fix it. If every one of those churches would reach 1000 people, which is unlikely, that's still just 100,000 people.

That's just .03% of our nation. Not three percent. Three hundredths of a percent. Not even a drop in the bucket.

A pastor emailed me the other week.

"I hear that you and Jeff and Bryan have church planting pretty much covered in Pennsylvania, so I'm asking myself, 'What's left for me to do?'"

Jeff Leake is planting his 9th church.

I've got a tiny little number in the can, approximately 20 churches that we helped plant.

Bryan might have 7 or 8. I don't know exactly.

And this young pastor thought we had the entire area taken care of.

"Where in the hell did you get that idea?" I wrote back to him – I chose those words because that's where an idea like that comes from. "That's not even close to reality."

"Well, maybe there's room for me to help revitalize existing churches," he conceded.

"Great. Okay, now I'm back with you. If you can find a way to revitalize churches that are dying, then that's a great mission."

But my mind churned. *How could a young pastor be so easily discouraged from planting churches when so little of it is actually going on in our country? What would make him believe that, in a heavily unchurched society like ours, two or three other pastors could have church planting sewed up?*

Then I read something by Dr. Ed Stetzer in Outreach Magazine that got my attention:

"Seems to be that churches must be on some powerful birth control. They are not reproducing. And I don't get why."[2]

We won't let ourselves grow.

If church planting is going to become a movement in our day, he went on to say, half of our churches have to be planting new churches. Half. Any less than that and we're just treading water. But the mainline perception is way off – just look at the young pastor's perspective that because three of us are planting churches, there's no more room. The younger generation sees all the old church buildings and believes the work is done. But those buildings are often very empty.

Somehow we have all been fooled into believing that it's time to maintain, not time to grow. Instead of planting new churches, we should just mow our grass and clean the windows and take out the trash.

This could not be further from the truth.

If we are going to prevail, we must plant churches.

Our church is a member of the Assemblies of God, hailed as one of the fastest growing denominations in the country. At first you say, "Yeah! Great news! That must be cause for celebration, maybe a little egocentric bragging, right? No? What could be wrong with belonging to the fastest growing denomination in the country?"

Dig a little and you'll discover this is not such a prestigious accolade, because no one else is growing. In fact, we garnered this honorable status by growing 2%.

In fact, just under 2%.

And this is one of the fastest growing denominations in the United States.

We'd have to be here for another five hundred years to make even the smallest dent! 2% growth on an average of 17% church attendance is miniscule. Ever since I've been in this particular district of the Assemblies church, from the early 1990s, it seems that we've had 360 churches. We close 8 or 10 a year and we open 8 or 10 a year.

The church as a whole is losing, and I'm convinced it's because we've fallen away from the brilliant leadership teachings of Jesus in Luke 10, where he sent out his disciples to the neighboring towns and villages. Most of us don't care about planting churches anymore. Most of us are abrasive instead of loving. We forget the harvest is ripe, and we have stopped going to the Lord of the harvest.

We have stopped trying to conquer new ground - instead, like the pioneers, we've circled the wagons, striving for a place where we can be protected. Our primary concern is with the horrible savages out there trying to decimate our church and change our country. But who are we fighting?

We are fighting against new churches.

We think new churches are going to steal our people. We think they're going to cause our offerings to dwindle. We think they'll poach our youth directors and children's workers and worship leaders. We can't allow one new church to start in our community because we're scared it will put us out of business.

This is ridiculous, but even more so when you look at the fact that well over 83% of people out there don't attend church regularly! Yes, there are plenty of folks out there to support a huge increase in the amount of churches. Five churches could open on my street and all six of us would do just fine.

When a team is losing, the coach has to take them back to the most basic of skills and rebuild the foundation. A losing team is losing because it does not execute the basics well.

Those basics can be found in Luke 10.

The last ten district councils I've attended within my denomination have failed to address church planting. We battle over the tiniest piece of doctrine – recently we fought over one word in a doctrinal statement for three hours. One word! Yet I can't remember one single agenda item during that council that had to do with the 83 lost sheep – the 83% of people who are not attending church on a regular basis and do not know Christ.

And the worst part is, it's my fault: I don't have one single, solitary idea to offer. I'm worse than anyone. I can see the problem, but I have nothing to offer. That makes me sick, and I don't know how to fix it.

Last year during my prayer time God told me: "Take courage: in one day, in one moment, I am going to give someone an idea that will get this country back to God."

That gives me hope.

In the meantime, does anyone else out there care about these lost sheep? Eight out of ten people you see on the street are lost. This is having a terrible effect on our community, our churches, and the kingdom of heaven.

This realization came on my saddest day. But there is a light at the end of this tunnel.

It's found in Luke 10.

Chapter One: A Mindset of Plenty

"His instructions to them: The Harvest is so great"

Luke 10 is a staff meeting with Jesus. He rounded up his disciples, was about to send them out, and wanted to give them some foundational concepts that would help them influence people for the kingdom of heaven. He's about to expose them to introductory, yet profound, concepts of leadership and church planting.

What's the first thing he says?

"The Harvest is plentiful."

There is a lot of great stuff out there about leadership these days, but while there are many leaders with many opinions, Jesus changed the world! His ideas about leadership are far beyond anyone else's – just look at the results. His radical teachings overthrew the greatest empire on earth within 100 years!

Jesus knows something about leadership, and his first concern is that I, as a leader, see a plentiful harvest.

I struggle with this. It has taken years of re-training by the Holy Spirit for me to get even a little bit of this concept, because I don't naturally see the harvest as plentiful. Truth is, I often see the world around me as not wanting to hear the message of the gospel. I tend to see the harvest as meager.

On the farm where I grew up, I marveled at my dad's ability to see the harvest. He watched a field of wheat grow and develop. To my young eyes, one green plant looked identical to the others. I didn't see the gradual changes day after day as the wheat went from green, to sprouting heads, and then to changing color! I missed what was happening right in front of me as the "fields became white unto harvest". I was too busy playing, living in the moment, and chasing fun, to see the opportunities that my dad's more disciplined, trained eye could see. When Dad announced that the harvest was ready, I was always amazed!

Young leaders, like young farmhands, must be trained to see that everybody wants to know God. It's not something we see naturally. It's not something the world will teach us. But it is a vital way of looking at the world. Otherwise, you'll find yourself mindlessly swinging the harvesting sickle at random plants. You may be working hard, but if you can't see the harvest you won't accomplish much.

I hate days like that.

I've had my share of them.

There are days when I spend hour after sweaty hour working hard but harvesting little, and there are days when I have swung my sickle but only collected a useless pile of grass and not the precious crops I went out to harvest.

The first concern of Jesus, the master of all leaders, is how you see the world. If you see the world abundant with harvest, you'll probably bring in some crops. If you see a meager harvest, you'll be left staring at a pile of grass.; In fact, anywhere that you see an abundant harvest, you will lead.

This is the closest Jesus got to using the word "vision", because at the heart of the statement "the Harvest is plentiful" is a question: What do you see? There were at least 8 or 9 leaders in the Bible who received a similar challenge regarding vision:

In Exodus 16:4 God told Moses, "**Look**, I'm going to rain down food from heaven for you."

Mark 1:2 entreats us to expand our vision: "In the book of the prophet Isaiah, God said, '**Look**, I am sending my messenger before you, and he will prepare your way.'"

Jeremiah 1:11 says "The word of the LORD came to me: '**What do you see**, Jeremiah?'"

In Ezekiel 8:15 we read that "He said to me, '**Do you see this**?'"

In Amos 7:8: "And the LORD asked me, '**What do you see**, Amos?'"

In Zechariah 4:2 "He asked me, '"**What do you see**?'"

What do you see?

Jesus wants to know: How do you see the world?

When he tells the disciples that the harvest is plentiful, he is trying to emphasize that there are people all around them who want to enter the kingdom of God, but these people need someone to show them the way. There are so many people seeking the kingdom of God! If we can see the world the way Jesus was telling his disciples to see the world, we could help bring in the harvest.

I recently took a trip to Nepal with Johannes Amritzer for a crusade. It can be hard for us to visualize here in the United States, with our shopping malls and sporting events and plummeting church attendance, but in other parts of the world the ripe harvest is so much more apparent.

No matter where we went in Nepal, people were desperate to experience the kingdom of God. Crowds of people desperate for healing would gather around our vehicles, trying to stop us from leaving because they wanted so badly to experience God. They wanted to see one more sick person experience healing. They were determined to experience God's kingdom here on earth.

Jesus is telling us today that if we don't see America as ripe for harvest, we will lose it all.

This is where some of us fall into the trap of resisting church plants – we can feel threatened. Satan tempts us into believing that there is no additional harvest in our neighborhoods, that we've maxed out on getting more people from our communities, and that there's no one left to start coming to our churches.

Recently, a pastor approached me when he heard we were starting a church in his area.

"Why are you planting a church in this area?" he asked. "I've got this town."

He had 48 people in his church and had been at that number for decades. He was concerned that if we came to his town we would take his people and lead to the closing of his church.

"You're not even reaching one percent of the people in your community," I protested.

"But I'm reaching the people that WANT to be reached," he said.

What this pastor didn't see is that so many people want to get into the kingdom of heaven, but we've found ways to keep them out! We've found ways to discourage them from coming to church, ways of making them feel that the kingdom of God doesn't work on their behalf, ways of making them feel that it is useless to try.

Job one for every leader is providing vision.

My son came to me and said he wanted to run our youth group. He was 17 at the time.

"What do you see happening in our youth group?" I asked. "What is the potential that you see?"

"We're averaging 40 kids," he said. "We should be averaging 200."

"Whoa!" I said – I had been expecting some optimism, but not downright delusion. "200? How are you going to reach 200?"

"I'm not sure yet," he said, "but here's the deal. I'm starting to see a picture of the way we could do things that might lead to 200 kids coming every week."

"What? I don't see that picture," I said, still a little hesitant.

See, I didn't want him to get discouraged. I didn't want him to aim for 200 and then, when he didn't hit it, give up. I wanted to protect him.

I saw maybe 60 kids coming out.

"You really think you can do 200?" I asked.

"That's the picture I see," he said, shrugging his shoulders.

Eight months after our discussion, youth attendance reached 120. So he went from sometimes as low as 40 a week to 120 a week. He added programs, gatherings, group activities. We count each person once, no matter how many times they come in a week, and he's up to 120 individual kids each week.

Now I can see the picture. But he's the leader, because he saw 200 when everyone else saw 40.

In every case where you see abundance, you are the leader.

Jesus asks, "What do you see?"

"How do you see it?"

"What is it that you are seeing?"

In every case in scripture where he asks this question, his point is that wherever you see abundance, you will be the leader. If you don't see abundance, you aren't leading. Vision is the ultimate, essential core of leadership, because if you can see abundance somewhere, you will lead in that area.

"Where do you see a mindset of plenty?"

Let me tell you a story of how this recently played out at our church. It was a typical board meeting. Someone, out of the blue, said something like:

"We ought to be reaching people with addictions in our community."

We looked around at each other with eyes wide open and doubt creeping on to our faces.

"How do we do that?" someone asked.

The first model that came to mind was the Teen Challenge model – they are immensely successful and have been working for years with people who struggle with addictions. But Teen Challenge usually has a large building or complex of buildings in an inner city, each of which typically house at least 40 or 50 people recovering from addictions.

If that's what it takes, then we didn't have the money.

A mindset of lack crept into our discussion. Suddenly we focused on what we didn't have – enough money to build a complex, enough volunteers to tend to the people, enough time to organize it.

Not a mindset of plenty. There wasn't one thing about our conversation that focused on what we *did* have, what we *could* do. We only thought, *We don't have what it takes to do that.* And the whole roomful of people squelched down and pushed the life out of that idea. *Great idea, but we can't do it.*

Then we were invaded by a solitary mindset of plenty.

"I'm thinking of getting an apartment," one of the single guys on our board said. "I don't know how I can afford it – I've got a minimum wage job. Let's forget the Teen Challenge model for a minute. That's too big for us. But what if I take the two guys in our church who are struggling for freedom, and I invite them to live with me. They can help me with rent, maybe pay $150 per month. It'll be the best deal they ever got."

He had our attention.

"And I'll show them how to live for Jesus," he concluded.

The room got quiet. I could feel the air coming back into the meeting.

"That might work," someone said, still talking quietly, probably in case they were the only ones who saw the promise in this new idea.

Suddenly we had a mindset of plenty, and we could accomplish anything. When that young leader said he could take two guys in his apartment, everyone's antennae went up. We got excited.

"What if we rented a bigger place?" someone else suggested.

"If you're willing to live in a place and pay $500, what if we rented a place that had three or four bedrooms and the church paid the difference, and you could help five or six guys?"

Then someone else spoke up.

"Hey, I've got a place I'm trying to rent out. I'm asking $1150 for it, but I'll rent it to the church for $1000. It's got 2 ½ baths and four large bedrooms. You could put three or four guys in each bedroom."

Silence again. In the matter of a few moments an idea that had no hope suddenly filled the room with anticipation. We suddenly had a mindset of abundance. We had an infusion of vision. We had a way to pay for it. All of that came from one guy down at the end of the table with the belief that he could do something instead of nothing.

Seeing the harvest as plentiful is everything.

Having a mindset of lack is something that I struggle with. It infiltrates almost every area of my life:

I don't have time.

I don't have enough money.

I don't have the right relationships.

I don't have the opportunities.

I don't have connections.

Whatever the perceived need, I probably just don't have it.

Most of my church board meetings are filled with people bringing up ideas and then me infusing a mindset of lack.

"Well, that's a great idea, but we just don't have the budget for that this year." That's most board meetings. "We don't have time for that" or "we don't have a place to do that" or "that's not simple enough – it's too complex." Whenever we as a board see lack, we can't function.

Many years ago my mom was fighting cancer.

"This is as bad a case of breast cancer as I've ever seen," the doctor said.

"Are you saying she doesn't have very much time?" I asked.

"I don't like to predict people's lives like that. I'm not God, and only God knows. But let me put it to you this way: if you ever wanted to say something to your mother, now is the time to do it."

My jaw dropped.

"You mean today?"

"Not just today. Before you leave this room."

I was blown away. Some of our other family members were in the room, too, and it got quiet. We all just sat there in stunned silence. I didn't know what to say or do.

But then my mom spoke up.

"Aren't you the one that believes in healing?" she asked me. "Get over here and pray for me!"

My mom walked out of that office with her shoulders back and a firm look in her eye.

"I'm never going to see that doctor again," she said. "He sees me dead."

"What do you mean, Mom? He's your doctor."

"I don't care who he is, if he doesn't see any hope why would I keep going back there?"

She had more of a mindset of healing (God's plenty) than I did at that point.

She lived for more than fifteen years after that prognosis of lack, and I'm convinced it was because she saw plenty: plenty of healing, plenty of life, plenty of God.

So why do so many pastors get upset when they hear that a church is being planted in their area, or their town, or on their street?

They have a mindset of lack.

Soon after our church took the huge step of buying land (and took on more debt than I could imagine), we put up a sign that said "Future Home of Freedom Valley." We were so excited. Finally we had our land and a building was coming.

Within what seemed like weeks, there was a sign next door saying, "Brand New Church: Adams County Bible Church."

Driving by their sign, I nearly choked on my coffee.

How could they do that? We weren't even on our land yet! We didn't even have the money for a building! We were only seven years old, and these people have the gall to open up next door! How could they do that? Were they trying to put us out of business?

13

I started coming up with all kinds of reasons why their presence would lead to our failure. All of my arguments were rooted in a lie: there were only 150 people in our community who wanted to enter the kingdom of God, and I had already found them, and now this new church would steal them from me.

The lie of lack.

It took all the self-discipline I had to keep from going nuts about that Bible church opening next door.

Not much later another church down the road built an addition, just as we were trying to build our first building on our new property. It was at this time I read somewhere about competing franchises, that when a Burger King opens up next to a McDonalds both stores do better than if they were standing alone. This challenged my thinking.

Thinking in terms of plenty is difficult for everyone, and pastors are not exempt from this challenge. We have so many bills to pay, and often a mortgage pressing in on us. But sometimes you have to force yourself to think in terms of plenty.

Last year we gave around $6,000 in tithes each month by sending out some of our church people to various new churches we were starting, but our income still ended up higher per month when compared to the year before. We went into that period of time struggling, wondering how we could lose those families and still make our budget. But I knew we had to overcome this mindset of lack – it takes such discipline!

If we can spend our time with God asking him to teach us in terms of plenty, just as Jesus was trying to train the disciples to think this way in Luke 10, everything will flourish.

I often struggle with the concept of prayer – Jesus says, "Your heavenly father knows what you need before you ask." Then why pray? Why even bother? Because it's not God that is the issue – it's me. In prayer I'm disciplining myself to be open to God-thoughts when it comes to plenty. Spending time in prayer helps me to see and believe in a plentiful harvest.

Everything changes when you have a brief morning meeting with the God who lives in plenty. He's not limited by my small ideas, or my pressing bills. He's not intimidated by the number of soldiers on the opposing side, or the impossibility of the task. He loves the come-from-behind win of one little guy who has the courage to believe that a big God can equalize any apparent disparity. In fact, He seems to take extra delight in making the impossible happen, and turning the underdogs into winners.

To pray an endless list of requests designed to get God to do things, while we sip another iced tea under the shade tree, misses the point. But to spend time with him, practicing His thoughts of abundance and imagining what it's like to stand with him on the winner's podium, in spite of unbelievable odds against us, can be time well spent.

That is the purpose of prayer.

When I spend time in the presence of the God-of-Abundance, I have enough time to do everything I need to get done, enough money to pay for it, and enough energy to enjoy it. Time with Him renders me more brilliant than my IQ explains, and more talented than anybody knew. It causes me to look good (confidence is the most attractive quality of all) and walk tall. It makes me immune to temptation because I believe God will take care of my needs in His character: abundance.

A little time with someone who believes in my ability to influence the world for good, and I am thinking those thoughts too. On the other hand, a little time contemplating what I do not currently have, and I become frozen with fear and doubt.

It is interesting that we, the church, who claim to be close to this God-of-plenty, are often the first to use His own scriptures to explain our unbelief and doubt. We teach one another to accept our inabilities, rather than strengthen ourselves to overcome. Our use of scripture is not unlike the devil's own, who used scripture wrongly to tempt Jesus into giving up his calling, and taking an easier way out of his future.

We tend to speak more of "doing leadership wisely" than we do about simple obedience and courage. It is interesting that the standard foundations of wisdom are often caution and safety, both of which keep us from taking over the world with this powerful gospel. Caution and safety keep us from taking any real risks. Is this true wisdom, or fear masquerading as wisdom?

The heroes of Acts seemed to take nothing but risks. If people rejected the truth they proclaimed, they believed God would use that situation. If they were told to be silent, they prayed for courage. If they were killed, they believed God could raise them from the dead. Their indomitable faith oozed out of every pore, and rendered them an impossible force to stop.

We have to learn how to think plentiful thoughts.

Chapter Two: Letting Things Fall Apart

"...but the workers are so few..."

Based on our last chapter, this might be difficult to comprehend.

Didn't I just talk about how important it is to have a mindset of plenty? Yet, in Luke 10, Jesus says the workers are few. Is he acknowledging a lack?

He is, but the lack of workers he is talking about doesn't affect the availability of the harvest. Just because the laborers are few doesn't mean that the harvest has diminished. The harvest is still plentiful.

By saying "the laborers are few," Jesus is inferring that there are things that will keep the plentiful crop from being harvested. A visionary like Jesus realizes that, even though the harvest is plentiful, it's not going to just walk into your barn. And sometimes it's not fun – sometimes it's sweaty and hard and takes a long time. But it has to be done.

In Nepal I asked myself almost every day, *Why am I out here? I could be reaching people in Gettysburg! Why did I come out here, and what do I expect to accomplish here? ? I can't speak the language. I'm never going to see these people again in my life! How does it count? How does my* *presence make a difference? And besides, it cost me $2,000 to get here. I could have done so many more productive things with that money in the community that I have been assigned to by God. Why am I not doing that?*

So I was asking myself all of these questions.

But here's the deal: Jesus said there is a lack in his kingdom, and the lack is laborers. And for the time that I was in Nepal, I was a much-needed laborer. The willingness of my team to work connected with God's willingness to move among people who desperately needed Him to do so.

I will not bring in a harvest if I cannot see it, so Jesus starts there, urging us to see it, and teaching us what it looks like. But then He also makes it clear that if we can see it, we will also need to work hard to bring it in.

One Sunday morning I challenged my congregation to start inviting people to church. I was serious. God was impressing on me just how plentiful the harvest was, and how few the workers. I wanted to motivate my people to get involved, to get out into the ripe fields.

This is a message that resonates with every serious believer in Jesus. There were many hearty 'amen's' as I talked about God's passion for people who feel confused, disconnected, and unloved. I felt like I had delivered God's heart.

But at the end of the service, I offered to pray with anyone who wanted to reach someone who did not have a relationship with Jesus. Based on the enthusiastic verbal responses while I preached, and the big smiles and nods of affirmation, I expected many people eager to pray the prayer of agreement with their Pastor.

No one came to receive that prayer.

I was disappointed, but I was also pretty confident that the lack of response was more about my relative inexperience as a communicator, not about their hearts rejecting the message. Anyway, after that particular service, I began to busy myself with the things I needed to do before I went home for the day.

As I worked at my after-service duties, a young boy came up to me, probably 5 or 6 years old.

"I'm going to start inviting people to church," he said.

I smiled politely, but inside I was thinking, *This is not the type of worker I had in mind. I want to invade the offices in our county, the workplace, the bar scene. I don't know how this little kid can be a serious player in the kingdom. He's just so young.*

"You do that," I said, humoring him.

"Will you pray with me about it?" he asked.

I said a short little prayer asking God to please help Evan invite someone to church.

I am ashamed of my mindset now.

What was I thinking?

Each day, Evan's mother picked her son up from school. One day, while she was waiting in her car outside the school, someone knocked on her window. It kind of startled her, and she rolled her window down.

"Hi?"

"Hi, are you Evan's mom?"

"Yes, I am," she said. "Uh-oh, what did he do?"

"No, it's nothing like that," the woman said, smiling. "Your boy and my boy play together on the playground, and we love that. But your son asked my son a question that he couldn't answer."

"Oh no, what has Evan been saying?"

"No," the lady smiled. "Don't worry about it. My son said that he and Evan talked about God. Then your son asked my son if he is a Christian. And my son said, 'I don't know. I'll ask my mom.'"

Evan's mom's eyes went wide open.

"To be honest," the woman continued, "I don't know what to tell him. Mostly I tell him that we live in a Christian nation, and our family isn't Muslim or Buddhist, so that makes us Christian, but I'm not sure if that's right. Is it?"

Evan's mom tried to answer.

"No," she said. "Not really. There's a lot more to it than that."

"I thought so. Is there any way we could just come over to your house and ask you some questions about it?"

"Sure," Evan's mom said. "I don't know what we're doing tonight, but we'll make it work. Come on over."

The family ended up coming to our church, all because one young boy decided to join in as a worker for the harvest. He asked one simple question, "Are you a Christian?" And it changed the lives of a family.

The harvest is plenty. The laborers are few. Will you be a laborer?

One Sunday morning, soon after our church moved into a little hole-in-the-wall location, I walked in to find a prayer group gathered around the back of the main room. A circle of 7 or 8 people held hands, praying. Immediately these stupid little thoughts started going around in my head: *Who authorized this meeting? What are they praying about?*

These are just some of the thoughts that the enemy tries to send into the mind of a pastor, thoughts that stir up feelings of insecurity and doubt. Why would prayer have to be authorized?

Anyway, I went over in an odd state of mind and joined the circle. Mark Keller, our worship leader at the time, was praying.

"God, if there's anyone in Adams County this morning that's feeling down and suicidal and doesn't want to live any more, could you send them here? We know how to help them."

Again, my brain resisted.

I don't have any time for another one of those! I already have three suicidal people I'm trying to mentor! I don't have the energy for one more — you bring someone else and I'll be suicidal! Don't pray that prayer, Mark!

Of course I didn't say anything, but that's what went through my head.

So the service started. Everything seemed like a usual church service. In those days we ended around noon. But at 11:45am, the back door opens and a couple walked in. They were well older than I, probably in their late sixties.

They just stood in the back, which was kind of awkward because our building wasn't put together to be a church, so there wasn't the normal entry way or foyer, just a door leading directly into the place we met. And they just stood there.

I finished the service and did an altar call to live out some part of the Bible I was teaching about that day, and some folks responded. I dismissed the congregation, prayed for those who came to the front, and at about fifteen minutes past noon looked up, only to find that the older couple was still standing at the back of the church, beside the doors.

Finally I went back to them.

"Hi, I'm Gerry. I'm the pastor here. Who are you?"

"I'm Howard and this is my wife April," the gentleman said. He was dressed in a good-looking suit, and she was equally well-dressed.

"Nice to meet you – what can I do for you?"

"Can we talk in private?" he asked.

He and I walked to the other side of the sanctuary – it was a 60-seat sanctuary, so it wasn't a very long walk! We sat down in some of the seats and April stayed at the back. Howard pulled a crumpled piece of paper from his suit, opened it and handed it to me.

"This is the suicide note I wrote this morning," he said. "This was going to be the morning I died. I got up this morning thinking about how I'm on my fourth marriage, my wife doesn't know I've cheated on her. My kids hate me. I keep thinking I'm not going to do it again, but I do. I give up! I have nothing."

"Okay," I said slowly. "Then why are you here? You were going to commit suicide but you obviously didn't."

"I am the chairman of the board at my church," he began.

"Then why did you come to this church?"

"My wife gets up far earlier than I do to get ready for church," he continued. "I decided that gave me enough time to kill myself. I was up all night thinking about it – I'm depressed out of my mind. So when she went to the bathroom to shower, and I heard the shower running, I started taking pills. I wrote this note."

"So what happened?"

"Well, I had the first handful of pills in my mouth, and a voice came to me. Pastor, I need to know, do you believe that God talks to people?"

I paused for a moment.

"Didn't you say you're chairman of the board at your church?" I asked. "Don't you read the Bible?"

"No, no," he said. "I know all the stories. But I'm talking about today. Do you believe that God talks to people today?"

"Yeah," I said. "I think God speaks to everybody."

"No! That thought creeps me out. I thought God was a concept, that we can talk to in heaven."

"Why don't you just tell me what happened? Not all voices are from God – the Bible says that Satan comes as an angel of light. Tell me what happened and I'll see if I can discern what kind of voice you were hearing."

He looked hesitant, then continued.

"A voice came to me, as I had that first fistful of pills, and said, 'Go to Debbie's church.' It freaked me out. I was wondering how I could already be hallucinating, since I hadn't swallowed many pills yet. So I started taking more pills and drinking water, but the voice came to me again and said, 'I said, go to Debbie's church.' I thought the first one was just my imagination, but the second voice was loud and insistent and demanding. So I went to the bathroom and asked my wife if we knew a Debbie."

"No, I don't think so."

"C'mon, honey, I need to know," he asked her again.

"There was that Debbie in the lawyer's office when we closed on our new house. Remember that? And then I saw her in the grocery store last week."

"Tell me about her!"

"That Debbie told me she is going to a brand-new church. Her marriage was on the rocks, but they found hope there."

"We have to find that church!" Howard said.

"All I know is that it's on Route 30 somewhere," his wife replied from inside the shower.

They drove from Thomasville towards Chambersburg, nearly 25 miles, and couldn't find us. Finally, on their second trip through they saw our tiny sign – we hadn't been approved by the township for a sign yet, so we just had something small out along the road, in the weeds.

Anyway, when they found us, they drove into our parking lot. Then they drove right back out.

"At first I told my wife, 'There's no legitimate church that would meet here. They must be a cult.' But we changed our mind and came in. We're here. Give me what you got."

"Do you have a relationship with Jesus?" I asked him.

"I go to church," he said with indignation.

"That's not what I'm talking about. Judas went to church. I want to know if you know Jesus. Have you accepted him as the boss of your life?"

"I guess not," he said. "I don't even know what you're talking about."

"Let's start there."

"Fine. I'll take whatever you have."

So he made a commitment to follow Jesus right there.

Then his wife came over, wondering what was going on.

I explained it to her, and she also made a commitment to Christ.

He wept and wept. They're still married today.

Eventually I looked up from praying with them and there was only one other person in the building: Mark Keller, standing at the back of the building, just waiting.

"Mark, what are you still doing here?" It was probably 2 or 3 in the afternoon by then.

"That's the suicidal I prayed for this morning, isn't it?"

I got chills.

"Actually, it is."

You see, Mark was a willing worker in the harvest, and God honored his willingness. He was ready. He was there to help.

"I want to invite them to our house for lunch."

Howard and April went to his house, not only for lunch, but for dinner, too. And not just Sunday night, but every night that week for two weeks. Every night.

Other people approached Mark and wanted to be part of this group – soon they had a home group of 30 people. They met every night for a while, then every other night, then once a week. It went on for two or three years.

Any place someone is willing to work, God has an abundant harvest waiting. And if they're not willing to work, the harvest will never be abundant.

I farmed for one year right after Julie and I got married. We were living on a farm in Quarryville, Pennsylvania before I went off to Valley Forge Christian College. The fall of that year my boss, who owned the farm, told us not to bother harvesting one of the corn fields.

"We've got to get out there and get that corn," I said one day.

"Nah, there's hardly anything in those fields. Probably not worth it."

A couple weeks later we were struggling to come up with enough grain to mix in to the cow's feed, so I brought it up again.

"There's plenty of corn," I said, "but it's just hanging out there on the stalk."

He waved his hand at me again.

"It's a lot of work, and it's a scraggly field. I'm just going to spend the money and buy what we need."

"What? It's right out there. We just have to go get it."

"It's not the worth the work. The field is low, and it's muddy. We'll wait until the ground freezes over, and then we'll go get it."

That year the ground didn't freeze until long into the winter. Every day past the optimum that you leave a crop in the field, more of it drops to the ground. And then, once you wait that long and come along with the corn picker, everything is so fragile that the rumble of the approaching tractor causes more ears to fall before you can harvest it.

I couldn't understand – why pay hundreds of dollars for feed, when it's right there?

"It's just too much work," he said.

Finally in February we harvested it. We got wagon-load after wagon-load out of that field, and we probably lost 40-50% of the crop at least, just because we waited too long.

We've got to bring in the harvest. It's always going to be hard work, and it's always going to require sweat and fasting and prayer. But if there's a worker, there will always be a harvest.

Sometimes, though, in today's big-church environment, there are a lot of people and not a lot of jobs. So what if you have workers but no place for them to work?

One of the most important parts of the ministry involves job placement – helping people find meaningful work within the church. This is one of the disadvantages of large churches – it can be difficult to find jobs for people, work where they see the harvest coming in. In a church of 50 you might have ten crucial leadership positions – this means that 20% of your congregation is immediately involved in work where they can see the harvest every week. But in a church of 1200 you might have 30 crucial leadership positions – now only 2.5% of the people are involved.

This is why planting new churches is so important.

I was at a seminar recently, and someone being ordained had the job title of "advanced middle school boy's pastor." My first thought was, *Wow, that's really segmented. How many pastors does this church have, that they're able to assign one person's full time ministry to boys in the 7th and 8th grade?* But here's the deal: this is a large and rapidly growing church, and they figured out a way to help someone have meaningful work.

Whenever we start a new church we send out teams – the point of teams is to provide meaningful work. So our teams consist of the following: worship leader, youth leader, small group leader, children's leader, hospitality person, outreach person, prayer person, senior pastor, and administrator. Once we get beyond those first nine positions, the rest take on the responsibility of being small group leaders.

When a group from our church left to plant a church in Tulsa, all 32 members of their group were leaders of something.

That's the key.

And now all of them will be out there bringing in the harvest.

All of them are laborers.

Recently I spoke with one of my church planters.

"Tell me about your schedule," I asked him.

"I'm putting 90 hours a week in at the church," he said, shrugging. "Plus I'm working a secular job."

I almost gasped.

"You're not going to live very long. You can't do that. Something's got to give. Tell me about what you're doing at church."

So he started getting into it, went on for a while about how he did pretty much everything.

"Maybe what you have to do is start getting other people to use their gifts," I suggested. "There's got to be some way that you can cut back your hours, because you're not going to survive much longer with that schedule."

He still didn't seem to be getting it.

"Oh Gerry, I'll be fine," he said.

"You're not even helping the church," I said, shaking my head. "You're hurting the church. You are killing the church, because you're doing all the work. That makes the laborers few. Everyone sees you running around and then they step back, saying, 'Just let him do it, he's better at it than me,' or 'Let him do it, because he's got the time.'"

"You don't have the time!" I continued. "You need to be focusing on your job as a leader."

"What's my job as a leader?"

"Find out where the abundance is! You've got to go back to point A. You've got to let your church work."

"Things would fall apart," he claimed.

"The best thing that could happen to your church would be for you to get sick and not be able to do anything for two weeks," I said.

"That's just mean," he protested.

"I don't think so. I think I'm trying to tell you that you are killing your church right now because you are not letting the laborers multiply. They are stuck and everyone is depending on you, and you feel really, really important and popular because all the fish and bread is coming from you, but what you're doing is keeping your church to the 40 people you can serve, every day."

Later I met with his people.

"Tell me what each of your spiritual gifts are."

This took some time, but eventually we figured it out.

"Okay, now tell me why you're not using your spiritual gifts."

"Pastor does it all," they said. "Those are his spiritual gifts, too."

"I doubt it," I said. "He's just doing this stuff to stay busy. His gifts are probably teaching the word or leading worship. But his spiritual gifts are not cleaning the church or evangelism or discipleship. There are a million things his gifts are not, and he's got to get out of those things, and you guys have to pick him up."

A young leader recently wrote me.

"I'm trying to train up another leader to take over some aspects of our ministry," he said. "But whenever I pull back, everything just falls apart. I can't pull back."

I thought about what he was saying and realized how important this was.

"You HAVE to pull back," I said. "Jesus sent his disciples across the lake and into a storm. The storm was strategic. He was trying to teach them that they can run a storm. They can administrate a storm. And, when you want to, you can tell the storm to shut up and sit down. Jesus knew the only way he could get them to understand this was to get them into a storm.

"So," I continued, "when you strategically pull back and everything falls apart, you're seeing it as a bad thing, but God sees it as a good thing. Because it causes the laborers to increase. How can I get you to see these storms as a good thing and not a bad thing? It's not your ministry going to hell – it's God raising up leaders. So let it go. Let it fall apart a little."

The fields are ripe for harvest.

Sometimes as a leader you have to push people to get involved. Sometimes you have to beg and plead and illustrate how their involvement can change the trajectory of someone's life.

But sometimes being a leader means you step back. You stop doing all the tasks that aren't in your strength, and you let things fall apart a little. Sometimes this, more than anything else, will draw people to participate in the harvest.

Chapter Three: Relying On George

"Pray to the Lord who is in charge of the Harvest..."

Where do you go when you lack something?

When life hands you a problem or a challenge or a seemingly insurmountable obstacle, who do you go to?

I think most of us, myself included, go everywhere but where we should.

We go to our spouses, our parents, our children, our doctors, our pastors, our friends. Some people go to their computers. Or their books. Or their addictions.

Some of us pastors run first to our people, or to our church pay check, or to the offering.

Why don't we go the Lord of the Harvest?

God began teaching me this lesson when I was still a young pastor. I relied heavily on my brother George for advice, council and wisdom. George and I had never been extremely close growing up; after all, there were 11 brothers and sisters in the family, and George was 18 years older than I.

In fact, it seemed to me that George was almost an outcast from our family because he left the Beachy Amish church that our family attended. Eventually I left, too, and started attending another church. One night, at this new church, a friend of mine came up to me.

"Hey," he said, "your brother George is here."

"No, I don't think so," I said, looking around.

"What do you mean, you don't think so?" my friend exclaimed. "That's him right there. That's your brother."

"Really?" I asked. "Are you sure?"

It had been so long since we had seen each other that I didn't even know what my brother looked like. That's how little I knew George at that point in my life.

"Come on over and I'll introduce you to your brother," my friend kidded me.

So we walked over. *Someone had better introduce me,* I thought, *because I don't even know that guy.*

"Hey George," someone said, "this is your little brother."

George kind of laughed.

"Yeah, I know him," he said, smiling.

Well, I barely know you, I thought.

Sometime later, probably after church, George and I were sitting around, just talking, and George started asking me questions.

"So tell me about yourself," George asked.

"Well, probably the biggest thing right now is that I have this call to ministry," I told him. "I hear you are a pastor, and I could use some help. I have no idea how this works."

From that night on he became my mentor.

So one night I called him, looking for some wisdom.

"I've got this thing I'm working on in ministry," I said, "and I have no idea how to handle it. Can you help me with this?"

George listened patiently and asked me a lot of questions. Then he prayed with me.

"I just don't know," he said, sounding confused. "God's pretty quiet. I don't know how to help you."

The phone line went silent for a minute as both of us were trying to think of a good way forward.

"By the way," George spoke up, "before you called me, did you pray to God about this?"

"Um, no," I said hesitantly, "I figured I'd call you first."

I was not prepared for the eruption I encountered. He literally screamed at me over the phone.

"DON'T YOU EVER DO THAT TO ME AGAIN! WHAT GOOD AM I TO YOU, IF YOU HAVEN'T ASKED GOD TO HELP YOU! The only good I can ever accomplish comes after you ask God to help, and then he can guide us. He might use me. He might talk to you without me, BUT DON'T YOU EVER CALL ME AGAIN WITHOUT ASKING HIM FIRST. PROMISE ME YOU'LL NEVER DO THIS AGAIN IN YOUR LIFE!"

I was shocked.

"I didn't mean to offend you," I sputtered.

"You didn't offend me!" he continued. "You wasted my time! I spent an hour listening to you and asking questions, when you didn't even have the decency to go to God first. He wants to be your source! He wants to be your big brother! You've got to get that. And if you don't get that, then our relationship is a waste of time!"

I just sat there, holding the phone away from my ear.

"I will never call you again without asking God first," I said, eyes wide open, feeling disciplined.

When I operate spontaneously, I talk to everybody else first.

I'll go to the board and say "We need more money." Or I go to my wife and say "How are we going to get this need met."

But what if I went straight to God? What if I went to him and said, "Lord, right now I could use some love," or "God, I really need another hundred dollars"?

What if I went to God and said, "Right now I'd really like to reach somebody"?

Why do I go to everybody else first?

This explains why Jesus said, "Ask the Lord of the Harvest." His point was that we go to every other source first! And every other source is good if you've gone to God first and asked him to guide your steps. But if you see other sources as first, God is likely to close up the heavens and wait – if he allows that other person to meet your needs, then you might not go to him in the future.

If he would have allowed my brother George to meet my needs that day, then I would have kept going back to him again and again for the rest of my life. For all of my answers. And George is just a person. He got that message through to me in a really big way.

James 4:2 says you do not have because you do not ask. He was saying there are a lot of Christians who never get around to asking God – they want things to happen, they even see abundance in places, but they "have not because they ask not."

"God, help us find laborers for the harvest field."

"God, help me see abundance."

"God, help me see the right abundance."

We've got to go right to that source, make our requests known to him.

But James also addresses something else: the double-minded person. I think in this context it is someone who asks God two different things. For example, I've known parents who've had rebellious children, and they've prayed, "God, either help my child to hit bottom so that they can begin following you, or bless them so abundantly that they know it has to be coming from you."

James says that when we ask we should believe and not doubt - a double-minded person won't receive anything from the Lord. I've discovered that most of the things I ask God for are double-minded, maybe even 99%. I would go to God and say, "Please either change that unruly board member's heart or get him off my board." When I'm asking for two things at once, not only am I letting doubt take over, but I'm also showing God that I'm more comfortable doubting than trusting.

And the Holy Spirit said, "Which do you want? I don't know which prayer to answer, and you wouldn't even know it if I did answer because you're not asking for one thing, you're asking for two opposing things."

"Well," I would reply, "ultimately I want him to have a better heart because he's a pretty good guy, most of the time, but he's been fighting me so much lately that it seems an easier solution for him just to be gone."

And the Holy Spirit came back to me again and said, "Then just ask that. Ask that! Ask that he receives a better heart."

So that's what I started praying, that this board member wouldn't be so argumentative, and wouldn't be so quick to anger, and wouldn't rely so heavily on criticism as a means of communication. I prayed that whatever had hurt him so deeply would be healed, releasing his heart from the pain that he was projecting on the rest of us. It wasn't long before this board member became one of my best helpers and most ardent supporters.

So I guess what Jesus and James are telling us is this: There is a right source and a right way, and doing one without the other isn't good enough. Go to the Lord of the harvest, and don't be double-minded.

If I go to God as my heavenly Father, which is what Jesus encourages, then I can walk right up to him and be bold.

"God, I want a million dollars," I might say.

God in his grace would tell me, "Gerry, you're not ready for a million dollars. You haven't handled the last $100 I gave you very well. So, no."

But I can still boldly ask. Hebrews says I should come boldly before the throne of grace. But asking isn't the best part. Asking just leads to further dialogue.

"Gerry, I WANT you to have a million bucks," God might say. "But right now you're not handling $100 very well - $1,000,000 would get you into so much trouble. Can I show you how to handle the $100 you have in a better way? And if you listen to me, then I'll show you how to handle $1000. Then $10,000. Then $100,000. Then $1,000.000."

See, if I never asked him for the $1,000,000, then this dialogue wouldn't have developed between me and God. Even though the request I had in mind was off base, God uses it as a tool to gently nudge me to the place I need to be. So ask boldly!

There was a lady at our church who had lost her husband. It was tragic, such a sad situation. One day, a few *years* after he had died, a conversation developed.

"I really feel the loneliness of your heart, and that hurts," I told her several years later, feeling the need to be up front with her.

"It hurts you?" she said, almost perturbed. "I'm the one that's lonely."

"I know," I said. "I know. Have you ever asked God for another husband?"

She sputtered and stammered, and I wondered if maybe I had crossed the line. Finally she got some words out.

"I just pray that I want the will of God. That's it. I just want the will of God."

I think that God wants our prayers to be bolder than that. I think he wants us to make big asks, and get involved in the Kingdom of Heaven that is among us.

"Wait a minute," I said to her. "What is *your* will?"

"I just want the will of God," she said with determination, not backing down.

"No, no, no," I said. "What do you want? Can you commit to wanting something?"

"No," she said, clearly growing more and more frustrated with me. "I just tell him I want his will. Whatever God's will is for my life, that's good enough for me."

I shook my head slightly.

"I think God's going to wait for you to decide what you want. I think the will of God is for you to have your heart. If my youngest daughter came to me when she was five or six and said, 'Dad, I'm hungry,' I would ask her what she wanted to eat.

Then, if she said, 'I'll take anything you've got,' I would go to the kitchen and get her a banana. Inevitably, when I gave it to her, she would then decide she didn't want bananas. So I'd get her some cereal. Well, that didn't look good to her either. If she didn't know what she wanted, anything I gave her would most likely not be good enough."

"My daughter would have to decide," I continued, "because I would gladly get her anything she wanted, as long as it wasn't bad for her, but she had to ask. Until she decided for herself, she wouldn't have accepted what I gave her."

She wasn't too sure.

When my associate pastor Marvin joined my team, he was 35 years old and single.

"Marvin," I asked him one time, "do you think you'd ever want to be married?"

"I don't know," he said, "I'm a really happy guy. I like my life and what God's doing. I just want the will of God."

"Marvin, maybe God waits for you to say what your will is."

"But I don't know what my will is," Marvin said. "My will changes all the time. Some days I think it would be nice to get married because it would be nice to have a friend. Some days I think it sounds like a drag, working at the relationship and having to make so many decisions together. I like my life now."

I had to concede to him.

"Maybe that's the perfect place to be. I don't think being content is a bad thing."

A few weeks later I spoke with Marvin again.

"You know," I said, "I've been praying for you, Marvin. And either one of those is the will of God – to be single is the will of God, and to be married is the will of God. What he wants is to know what you want."

Marvin got really quiet for a moment.

"I don't know what I want," he said.

"Why don't you make it your goal that by the end of this year to decide what you want?"

This discussion happened at some point in the summer.

A month or two later he came to me and we talked again.

"I think I'd like to be married," he said. "If it was the right situation, and if it was a beautiful woman that I could be great friends with, and we could be partners together in life, then I think I'd like that."

By the end of that year he was engaged.

I'm convinced that, for Marvin, this happened because he decided what he wanted. He wasn't double-minded anymore.

This is why Jesus said that God knows what we want before we ask – his knowing isn't the issue. The issue is our knowing! We have to know what we want! So when we're asking the Lord of the harvest, it is a process of decision-making. It's not becoming so holy that we suddenly think how God thinks. God will not decide for you what makes you happy. He gave you a marvelous brain to do that for yourself.

I learned this when I first became a father – it wasn't up to me to decide what made my daughter Candace happy. And even if I could have, I wouldn't have done it. If I would have tried to decide what made her happy, she probably would have turned her nose up at it.

Now when I go before God, I spend that time trying to figure out what my desires are.

I met with a church planter who was struggling with his calling.

"I am just not happy these days," he said.

This was a guy who had planted a church and watched it skyrocket in attendance almost immediately to 200 people.

"How can you not be happy!" I practically shouted. "You have every pastor's dream!"

"The bottom line is," he said, "I think I'm living your dream."

A hush fell over our conversation as we sat there, taking that in.

"I don't want to do this job," he said again, shaking his head.

"What do you want to do?" I asked, still taken aback.

"I want to be a counselor. The problem with my church is that almost all the people I've reached are happy. That's not my goal. I want to find unhappy people and help them discover happiness. I feel like there's no work for me here. There's nothing for me to do."

"When you pray, what does God tell you?" I asked him.

"God tells me to go find some unhappy people and bring them joy."

This guy discovered in his prayer time that he was in the wrong job – what he was doing was not his calling.

"We've got to find someone to fill your spot."

"I already did," he said. "I'm working with him right now. My associate pastor is dying to lead this church."

"Perfect," I said. "Now you have found what's going to make you happy, and he's going to be able to move into the role he's been dreaming about. This is a win-win situation. How soon can this happen?"

He shrugged.

"Probably in the next couple of weeks."

"Your people are going to cry a lot," I said.

"It's okay, I'll give them time."

When Jesus said, "Ask the Lord of the harvest", he was saying that the key to the harvest is to find out where your heart is, what will fulfill you in life, and to go after that single-mindedly.

I was talking with a young man just the other day.

"Tell me about your plans for your future."

"I can't decide. I'm so depressed right now. I can't decide."

Depression can sometimes be the direct result of not making a decision about what will make you happy: either you have not made a decision, or you don't know what to ask God for, or you don't know what to do with your day. Nothing you do brings contentment – not the best job in the world, not all the money in the world. You're still depressed.

Money, sex and power – you can have all of these in overabundance, but if you haven't decided what makes you happy, it will all mean nothing to you. What the world considers to be the big three would be worthless.

"A year ago," I told a young man, "you said you wanted to go to school. What happened?"

"I decided that's not going to make me happy. I don't even know how to pray anymore."

"But that is what you need to be praying: 'God, help me figure out what will make me happy.' You can pick a billion different things and God would say, 'Great, let's go for that.'"

"Ask the Lord of the harvest." Don't ask your board or your spouse or your kids or your pastor or anyone else.

Go to the Lord of the harvest with a single-minded approach.

Remember that story of the lady whose husband had passed away, and I challenged her to decide what she wanted? Well, she decided she wanted to be married again, and seemingly out of nowhere she met a guy who had just lost his wife. About a year and a half after that, she was a happily married woman.

"I'm so excited about this!" she told me. "God gave me not just one love, but two. I found such a good man – how do I deserve to be so happy twice?"

God wants you to experience joy.

Just go to the Lord of the harvest.

Then go into His harvest fields.

Chapter Four: The New Motorcycle

"Go now..."

2006 was the worst year of my life

There was so much hell going on around me – I got to the place where I just couldn't deal with it. It was unbelievable, and I started thinking about leaving the ministry. Every aspect of my life was under heavy attack – my marriage, the church, my health, everything. And in the middle of all of this I started getting pains in my chest.

I thought I was having a heart attack, and I went to the hospital.

"There's nothing wrong with your heart," the doctor said. "Your heart is in great shape. What's going on with you emotionally?"

I looked at him and got honest.

"I'm going through hell this year, in every category of my life."

I started listing off all the things that were troubling me.

The doctor nodded.

"It's your emotions, not your heart," he said.

That's when I knew I had to focus on getting these things right. The emotional stuff.

The hard stuff.

At the end of that year, when I saw how God was bringing me through it, I felt overcome with thankfulness. My vision for life came back.

"God," I prayed, "there is not a thing I own that's worth as much as having vision. I just want vision – when I have that, everything else comes easily."

Then it was almost like the Holy Spirit said, "Great. Let's prove this little concept."

Uh-oh.

"What if you give away your motorcycle?" I felt that little voice ask.

About this time I preached at a Sunday evening service, one of those times when God moved through the place with a fresh experience. One of my church planters, able to be there because their church didn't meet on Sunday nights, came up to me during the service.

"I feel that God is saying he's back in the house and it's time to slay the fatted calf, like when the prodigal son returned home."

Fatted calf, I thought to myself. *What's that?*

Oh.

It's my motorcycle.

That's the only fatted calf I owned. I was only able to buy it because of a gift someone had given me – I certainly didn't have it because I deserved it. And having my vision restored was worth way more than any motorcycle.

So I decided to give it away.

Then the Holy Spirit challenged me again.

"Do it publicly. Try me in this – in tithes and in offerings. See if I won't open up the heavens."

So, at church that night, I got up in front of everyone.

"I feel so privileged that God brought me through this year, and that he's blessed me with vision and hope and belief, that I'm going to give my motorcycle away."

I could feel the whole church gasping. They knew how much I loved to ride my bike. They knew how much that crazy piece of machinery meant to me.

Even my wife wasn't so sure.

"You've got to be kidding me! I love that bike!" she said the next day.

"Hey," I said, smiling, "this is my bike. Not yours."

"Yes, but I like it as much as you do.".

"Honey, just try to trust me in this."

And once again, she didn't waver.

"You know I trust you. If you want to give your bike away, give it away."

"Well, I don't really *want* to, but I will."

Truth is, I had suddenly received a weird 'want-to' when it came to giving away that motorcycle. I had never experienced anything quite like it before or since. Only God can give you a want-to for something like this. So within a month or so I sold my bike, paid the debt associated with it, and gave the rest to missions, as directed by the Holy Spirit.

"God told me to do this as an example of faith for everyone, so here's my check."

And I put it in the offering. Once again, a gasp from the crowd who knew how much I had loved that bike!

"We're going to watch God work," I said. "And if he doesn't work, you know, I don't need another motorcycle. I need passion and faith. I need God in my life. To heck with the bike – it's no fun anyway when you're going through a place where it feels like God isn't showing up. Anyway, I'm just so excited to take this step of faith and see what happens."

Two months before all of this went down I had planned a bike trip with the church for the end of January. But now I didn't have a bike.

"What about the bike trip?" everyone kept asking me. "What are you going to do?"

"I don't know."

41

"Are we just supposed to go without you?"

"Whatever you do, don't cancel it," I said. "I'm still planning on going." I still had this gift of faith about the trip. I just felt I would be there with them – either I'd borrow a bike, or something else would work out.

Let me tell you: something else worked out.

A few weeks later, a guy came up to me after church.

He looked a little bit emotional and was at the front of the church after everyone had left.

"You're Tom, right?" I asked.

"Yeah," he said. "I'm surprised you remember."

"I remember meeting you one time before, but I haven't seen you for a little while. What's going on?"

"Can I ask you a question? Have you ever thought about riding a motorcycle? I mean, do you know how to ride a motorcycle?"

Inside I was thinking, *Don't mess with my head, buddy.*

"That's not funny," I said, not entirely kidding. "I just gave my motorcycle away."

"You mean you owned a motorcycle?"

"Yeah! I just gave it away. You didn't hear my story?"

"I don't even know what you're talking about," he said.

"God just gave me this desire to give my motorcycle away, or sell it and give the money to missions, so that's what I did. So I don't have a motorcycle right now."

"Oh," he said, as if I had just explained much more to him than that simple story. "That explains it. I just got a brand-new motorcycle. And every time I ride it the Holy Spirit tells me, 'This is Gerry's bike. You need to go give him that bike.'"

"What? That doesn't make any sense," I said.

We just kind of looked at each other for a moment. I think both of us were a little startled by where the conversation was headed.

"Look, I've got some pretty specific parameters for what I'm looking for in a bike," I said. "First of all, I want a Harley."

"It is a Harley."

"I would like a Heritage Soft Tail."

"That's what it is."

"I've always sort of had my heart set on the '06 model."

I couldn't even believe I was saying what I was saying, and I certainly couldn't believe his responses.

"It is an '06," he said. "I just bought it. It has about 300 miles on it."

I took a deep breath.

"What are you saying again?"

He reached into his pocket and pulled out the keys.

"I want to give you my bike."

And he started peeling the key off the ring.

"Are you kidding me? Because this is not funny, if this is your idea of a joke."

At that point his wife came over.

"Are you just going to be miserable the rest of your life, or are you going to give Gerry your bike?"

"I'm doing it. Here's the key, right here."

"Good," she said. "Otherwise I don't want you to come home today. I'm tired of this whole discussion, and most of all I'm tired of you being miserable over your bike. Give it to him already."

"Okay," he said. "That's it."

And he started to give me the key.

"Now wait a minute," he said. "The bike could really use a servicing – there was a break-in period and I should send it back to Harley and have them get it ready for you."

Oh great, I thought. *He's taking it back and he's going to change his mind. He'll probably find a way to wiggle out of this.* I returned the key.

But on Wednesday morning he called me.

"The bike should be finished today. Let me know when you can get to the dealership and I'll meet you there to transfer all the paperwork."

"I'll be there at noon."

I walked into the dealership and immediately I could tell that all the employees were looking at me kind of funny.

"So you're the guy," the man behind the counter said.

"What?"

"You know this bike is worth a lot of money. Is he actually giving you this bike, or do you guys have some kind of a deal worked out?"

"No, he's giving me the bike."

"That's ridiculous! No one ever gives a bike like this away."

"I know! It's crazy!"

Do you have the courage to believe God and then act on whatever it is that he gives you? Sometimes he'll give you a lot and sometimes just a little. But the progression of commands is to ask the Lord of the harvest *and then go* into the harvest field. That's the principle we're working on here.

The asking has to be matched by some kind of movement toward it. It can be really simple: maybe the movement is to pray about it every day, or meditate on God's promises in that area of your life each day. Maybe the movement is to sell your own motorcycle. Whatever you do, figure out an act of faith and go for it.

I'm believing right now that I can be part of 1000 new church plants in my lifetime. How am I going to accomplish that? I have no idea. But the how isn't important. It's the what, and the fact that I believe God can make "the what" happen. And I'm moving forward in faith, planting as many churches as I can while God positions me to learn more and more about how the 1000 church goal can be reached.

Don't worry about how things will happen.

Ask the Lord of the harvest, and then go into the harvest field

Chapter Five: The Eater and the Eatee

"I am sending you out as Lambs among Wolves"

When I planted our church, Freedom Valley Worship Center, I felt like I was mentally prepared for a lot of challenges. I knew there would be difficulties and disagreements. I knew there would be people that tried to stop what I was doing. I figured on times when finances would be tight, both personally and in the church.

But the thing that I've realized in the last eighteen years is that the greatest opposition to new churches is not the world. For the most part, the world doesn't even care when a new church is planted. Sure, they might throw some zoning issues your way having to do with parking or the number of people allowed in a building. But the world pretty much sees new churches as harmless, meaningless, and even insignificant. Recently, we were working on yet another zoning issue and a lawyer, working for the local municipality, made the comment that "Zoning could safely be changed to accommodate Freedom Valley because it may be growing, but it's the only church in the world that is growing.

45

"Let's face it," he said. "Churches just aren't growing these days."

I clamped my mouth shut, but inside I was thinking; *You really gotta get out more, sir!*

Still, a new church will always run into opposition.

Wait, I hear you say. *You just said the world doesn't care — the world views a church plant as insignificant. If the world isn't opposing new churches, then who is?*

The greatest opposition we have ever faced, in all the churches that we have planted, has come from the unlikeliest of sources: the church.

I had been in New Oxford, Pennsylvania only a few days. We were still gathering together what would be the beginnings of our new church. We had moved into a small house with our three kids and were just getting settled in a new town. We had left what I believe to be one of the closest-knit communities in the United States, moved almost 100 miles away from our family, and, with no real security or assuredness that things would work out, started a new adventure.

We planted a church.

My wife, Julie, and I had been praying that I would find some kind of an outlet to begin interacting with the local pastors — during my time in Lancaster, I engaged in a pastor's fellowship, and it proved invaluable. Those fellow pastors helped me, encouraged me and strengthened me.

Seemingly out of nowhere, our prayer was answered when a local pastor gave me a call.

"Gerry," he said, "I hear you're new to the area. We have a pastors' fellowship we want to invite you to, and we want to pray over you and bless you."

"Wow, " I said, reminded again of the fellowships I had been part of in the past. I thought everyone was like Larry Kreider from Dove Fellowship, or Sam Smucker, pastor at The Worship Center. These men led one of the fellowships I had attended — I thought all pastors were encouraging and kind.

"When is it?" I asked.

He told me the date, which was the next week.

"We meet at the church for prayer for an hour or two, and then we go to a restaurant for lunch. This is a spirit-filled group — these are pastors that really care about the community."

"Great," I said. "I'll see you then."

I was hanging up the phone from that call when I felt the Holy Spirit say, "Don't go to that meeting."

Huh?

I went into the kitchen where Julie was, suddenly uncertain.

"Julie, you know how we just prayed that I would find some fellowship and be surrounded by guys that cared about me? This pastor just called and invited me to this meeting."

"That's our answer to prayer!" she said (probably unpacking or chasing our kids around the small house, or both).

"But I think, *I think*, when I was hanging up the phone, the Holy Spirit said, 'Don't go.'"

It felt almost strange, those words coming out of my mouth.

"That doesn't make any sense," she said. "But I guess you'd better not go, if that's what the Holy Spirit is telling you."

Guess what? I went. I just could not conceive of the Holy Spirit telling me not to go to a pastors fellowship. This had been something we were praying for, and it seemed too good an opportunity to pass up.

I walked into the church and met the pastors — there were five or six of them, all with churches in our community. The prayer time was fine. We prayed for the community, for the churches and their pastors, that sort of thing. Then it was time for lunch.

We shuffled into the back of a local restaurant and sat around a table. After we ordered, we sat there making small talk for a few minutes, and then the pastor who had called me on the phone spoke up.

"I'm sort of in charge of this thing, since this fellowship was my idea, so let me ask you some questions."

"Go for it," I said.

He picked up his coffee mug and held it up to his face, the steam rising up in a cloud as he spoke.

"Tell me about your vision for being here to plant this church."

There wasn't anything threatening in the question – in fact, I was so passionate about my vision for our new church that I immediately took those pastors to the heart of my calling.

"Well, God called me to reach people who have given up on church, and here's how I see it working. Some people have had really bad experiences, or have been hurt, or maybe they've done something stupid, or maybe they've offended the whole church. Maybe they just feel outcast. You know, there's that scripture that says "David gathered all the outcasts around him" and loved them. People who owed taxes, it says. I love that imagery. People who were outcast by their families and cast out of their city – David gathered them and loved them and gave them a community and turned them into an army.

"That's the picture God gives me," I said. "That's the picture that matters to me."

I was really getting into it, trying to convey my vision to these local pastors. But then the lead pastor stopped me.

"Hold on a second," he said, interrupting me. "Brother Gerry, I know you really want to help people. But I've got to tell you, that's the worst vision I've ever heard in my life."

I nearly fell backwards off my chair.

"Really? Why? Why is that so bad? I want to help people heal."

He put his coffee down and leaned forward.

"Can you imagine a place like that? Let me just tell you this," he said in a voice that left no room for discussion. "What do hurt people do. To each other."

These were not questions. They were statements.

"I'm not sure what you're looking for," I said. "Maybe they hurt each other?"

"Exactly! Hurting people hurt other people. They don't mean to, but they're grouchy and mad. Can you imagine a room full of these hurt, mean, grouchy people? That's not a place I want to be. I don't ever want to attend a church that's full of hurt people. It would be THE most painful place on earth, wouldn't it?"

I was still trying to catch my breath but managed to sort of moan out a "Yeah, I guess, I don't know."

The table was silent for a moment. The other pastors looked at me, convinced with the sound nature of this pastor's logic. Finally words came to me.

"I don't know why, but God inspired me to do this. I'm excited to be in that room. I WANT to be in that room of hurting people. God sent me to help them heal!"

But he wasn't going to back down.

"You're crazy," he said. "I'll tell you what – it will never work, you will fail, and, not only that, you'll fail painfully. That's what I believe. I want to save you from this – you've got to change your vision."

"Man," I said, "I could change my vision as easily as I could stop breathing. I'm sorry."

"Let me tell you some more things," he continued. "You don't know this community like I do. I've been pastoring here for decades – great stuff doesn't happen here."

"Really?" I exclaimed.

"You're not the first pastor that's come here with a vision. So did I. So did a lot of these guys. They all came here with a vision. We all had a vision from God, just like you. Haven't you noticed yet that there aren't any great churches here in this community?"

"Really?" I exclaimed again, my voice getting higher with each protest. "Yours isn't a great church? You've got 300 people! This guy's got 200 people. This guy's got 600 people. What do you mean, there's no great churches in this community?"

"Great churches don't happen here in the Gettysburg area.. You don't read books about churches in this community. Pastors here aren't writing books about making a difference. There is something evil about this community that kills you – if you're not ready for that, if you don't prepare yourself for that, you're going to be the most bitter, disappointed pastor of us all."

After a while I decided to just let him talk. He went on and on, and just when I thought that he was wrapping it up, the other guys started chiming in a little, telling horror stories of local pastors who hadn't made it, whose churches had gone under, whose ministries had failed. They told about how hurt those pastors were, how they ended up in mental facilities or had affairs, and how, in the end, the community had just chewed them up and spit them out.

It took me months to recuperate from that meeting.

Two weeks later.

I still remember the feeling inside of me when I heard someone pulling into our driveway that spring evening. My wife Julie and I were on an emotional roller coaster, one minute excited and passionate about starting our church because we genuinely felt that God had sent us there, and the next moment terrified and hounded by doubt.

Hearing someone's vehicle rolling over the loose stones beside our house gave a small lift to my spirits. The first two or three weeks we lived there, no one ever called us on the phone - I was even hoping telemarketers would call. I'm serious! I remember a telemarketer calling, and I remember the conversation, because I was so hungry for human interaction.

And now someone was actually visiting us.

"Somebody's in the driveway," I said.

I stood up from the dinner table and gave Julie a bemused shrug. Our three kids kind of looked out the window but just kept eating. It was pizza night at our house, and our house loved pizza.

"I don't know who it is," I said, answering her unasked question.

I walked out on to our small wooden deck behind the house, just off the tiny kitchen where we ate. Splinters stuck to my white socks, and I waited at the edge of the deck as a car pulled in and parked. A guy got out of his car, and I could see he had his family with him. He smiled when he saw me, waved and walked up on to the deck.

"Hi, I'm Gerry," I said, holding out my hand. "Who are you?"

"Hi Gerry," he said, and at first I couldn't place him, but he introduced himself as one of the local pastors. "I'm Ben."

"Good to see you," I said

"Beautiful day," the pastor said. "How are you guys doing?"

"This is great weather. We're doing just fine. What brings you out here?" I asked.

"Well, Gerry, I hear you're new in the community, that you've been sent here to plant a church, and I just want you to know that I'm so excited that you're here."

I felt this rush of emotion and thankfulness, and I wanted to hug the guy right there on my deck. Finally someone that didn't hate my guts, or think my vision was stupid! The meeting with the other pastors still hung around me like a cloud, so I appreciated this pastor's kindness – it met a deep need I still felt to somehow connect with the local pastors and spend time encouraging each other.

"That's just great!" I said. "Tell me about yourself."

"I pastor a church up the street, about ten miles away, and we are very happy that you are here in this community. Except one thing. I had a board meeting last night and we prayed for you."

"That is the most refreshing thing you could have told me. Thank you so much," I said, feeling more and more drawn to this guy. Here was someone who seemed to understand my need for connection.

"And God gave us a word for you," he said.

I was dying to hear it. I had already been told I was an idiot for planting in the Gettysburg area.. I had been told my vision was not feasible, unrealistic, even harmful to the church. I had been told I would mentally break down under the pressure, perhaps even go insane or have an affair. Finally someone who got it!

"I'm always up for a word from God," I said.

"The word might not excite you," he said cautiously. "The word God gave us was that you made a mistake coming to this community and you already regret it."

51

I froze, not knowing what to say. My eyebrows shot up. I thought he had just said that he was glad I was there! But I didn't have to say anything because he continued.

"I really admire your courage and the fact that you were willing to take this risk, and when God spoke to us it sort of stunned us, and we felt such compassion that we took up an offering. So here's $150 for you to move home. We don't want you to be stuck out here. We feel like someone deceived you into coming, and it's such a shame that you have relocated your family and moved and everything. So here's a check written out to you so that you can rent a truck if you want to move home. Call me if you want help to load your things."

Then he hugged me. Even though I didn't feel the need to hug him anymore.

I'll give him this – he was really caring in the way he spoke and seemed genuinely sad for me. He honestly thought he was helping me. I, however, was not feeling very helped.

For one brief moment in time, I paused. The shock just kind of washed over me, and in its wake was a feeling of sadness and resignation that yet another pastor in the community did not believe in my vision. But something in me was getting used to it, too. Something in me began to realize that if God's plan for this new church was going to take place in New Oxford, I was going to have to hold firm against all of this negativity and discouragement.

"I don't know how to tell you this," I said, reaching out and taking the envelope with the check inside (it did not pry easily from his fingers). "First of all, I want to thank you for this money. Just this morning Julie and I prayed that God would give us the money to have a pizza party for the neighbors so that we could get to know them. I believe this is that money."

He didn't say anything, but I thought that after I said what I was about to say, he might be just as stunned as I had been a few moments earlier.

"Second of all," I said, feeling a determination rising in me, "we aren't going anywhere. We're planting a church in this community, and we're here to see it through. God called me here

– I didn't get here on my own. I didn't dream this up. God brought me here. I want to be here with my whole heart. I put my family at risk. I'm not moving."

An awkward moment ensued as the spring dusk began settling around us, and I stood there holding the envelope. Finally he spoke, slowly, hesitantly.

"Well, okay Gerry, if that's how you feel. We just wanted you to know the word that God was giving us. I don't want to be a problem – I'm just trying to be faithful with what I think God said to me."

"I appreciate that," I said. "But most of all I appreciate the money. We needed the money."

The man turned and got in his car and drove away. The sound his car made driving out over the gravel was not as pleasant as it had been coming in – I was kind of glad to hear him driving away. I walked back inside. Julie looked up at me expectantly.

"Well?" she said.

I shook my head, once again in disbelief, and handed her the envelope.

"Here is the $150 that we needed for the pizza. But you will not believe this story."

I told her what the pastor had said, what his word from God was.

You know what she did? She just laughed a little bit.

"Well," she said, "at least we know that's not true."

If she had wavered at that point, I may have folded. All these pastors thinking we had made a huge mistake. But her support gave me a continued sense of resolve.

That first summer we were in New Oxford our church started with 42 people (many of which were family who had traveled in to support us). But even our own family members weren't exempt from the atmosphere of negativity surrounding us.

One family member, during our first day of church, pulled me aside.

"Glad we could be here," he said.

"Yeah, thanks a lot for coming out to our first service," I said. "It means a lot."

"We just thought, you know, if no one showed up, it would be a shame for you to go through it on your own."

"Wait a minute – you don't think this will work, do you?"

He kind of cleared his throat and shuffled around.

"Well, if it doesn't work, at least we were here for you."

I just shook my head in amazement, thinking to myself, *You came all the way here to support my failure? That's so nice of you!*

The messages coming at me that summer were so strong, messages that what we were doing would not work, that planting this church was unnecessary, or foolish. I even had one relative who asked me if I was planting a church because I wasn't good enough to get my own, established church.

What?

After the first few weeks, bolstered by the visits of family and friends, attendance dropped down into the twenties. On our lowest attended Sunday we had 19 people, but I remained encouraged – our core folks were strong, and I felt that we could build with them.

It was July or August, and the summer heat came through the door in waves whenever it was opened. On one particular Sunday I could tell something was wrong as soon as I walked in. The core group of people, as well as the couple who led worship, were all being very stand-offish towards me. There was a lot of whispering and averted eyes.

Finally I took the worship leader aside.

"What's going on here? I feel an undertow this morning."

He kind of looked around, like he was nervous.

"I didn't want to tell you this," he said. "Actually, I don't know how to tell you this."

"Lay it on me. C'mon, what's going on?"

"Last Sunday the pastor of the biggest church in the area held up a letter during the service and said, 'You know that new church you're hearing about in New Oxford? It's out of the will of God. The leadership there is in rebellion. Don't be part of something that God has cursed. This letter in my hand is from the overseer of that new young pastor over there in New Oxford and it proves that he is in rebellion to his own authority. God will not bless that.'"

"What are you talking about?" I asked. "How am I in rebellion?"

The worship leader shrugged.

"He had a letter right there in his hand, and he was holding it up, waving it at the congregation."

"I'm in rebellion? I didn't know I was in rebellion! What letter did he have?"

I was shocked to my toes. I walked over to my little office area just off the room where we met, and I slumped down in my seat.

"Lord," I prayed, "I cannot take any more of these hindrances from church people. What am I doing so wrong that causes the people, who should be on my side, to constantly attack me? I think I could take the attacks from the world, but this is crazy – this is coming from the church!"

How was I supposed to preach under this? I suddenly understood what all of those pastors had said at the fellowship, that I would leave New Oxford bitter and angry and burned out.

But I had to do something. I wasn't in any rebellion of which I was aware – we were getting financial support from our home church, from the Assemblies of God denomination, from individuals like Galen and Vern Smoker who sent us a check every single month for our first seven years. None of these folks told me I was rebelling. The guy I reported to in the Assemblies had not raised any issues with me.

The Holy Spirit rose up in me, gave me an idea, so I wrote out the name and phone number of my overseer on note cards.

Before the service I got up and mentioned that I heard about the local pastor's claim that I was in rebellion to my authority. I told those nineteen people that if I was in rebellion, I didn't know about it. Then I handed them each a 3x5 card.

"This is the man who is my boss. This guy authorizes the checks to be written from the Assemblies of God. His phone number is on there, too. Call him! Please, if you have any doubts about my actions, call him!"

They looked at each other, and I could tell that since I was being so open about it, they were beginning to believe there must a misunderstanding.

Then my worship leader spoke up.

"I'll call him tomorrow and let you all know."

I went straight home after church and called my overseer.

"Am I displeasing you in any way? Are you angry with me?"

I told him the story of the letter.

"Do you know what he's talking about?" I asked.

"I have no idea what he's talking about. You'll have to call him."

So the next day, in fear and trembling, I called the pastor who denounced me from his pulpit.

"Pastor," I said, "I met with you and you told me to start in New Oxford. I thought I was pleasing you and my overseer. What am I doing wrong?"

"Young man, that letter told me that you are going to start a church in New Oxford, and I've heard you are meeting in Gettysburg," he said.

"Wait a minute," I said. "I got a copy of that letter, and the letter tells me that New Oxford is one of the target communities, but anywhere in Adams County is fine. Is that not the case? Am I not welcome in Gettysburg?"

The intensity in his voice went up a level.

"The way I understand it, young man, you were charged with starting a church in New Oxford, it's the New Oxford church, and your church right now is meeting in Gettysburg. You are out of the will of God!"

"I am so sorry," I said. "I don't mean to be out of the will of God. We are meeting in Gettysburg because we couldn't find a place to meet in New Oxford. And here's what my overseer told me – he said 'you can start a church anywhere in this section.' That includes approximately five counties. In fact, he told me that across the street from his church would be a great place to start. He told me he's not reaching $1/10^{th}$ of 1% of the people in his community, and he wants more churches there! He told me there's not one city in our section that's off limits; there's not one area that's a bad area. We picked New Oxford because that's where we were looking at a house, so we named New Oxford as a possibility on that letter you mentioned."

The conversation ended cordially enough, but my heart was racing. It seemed that everywhere I turned, the church was providing so much opposition.

I experienced this kind of resistance throughout my first year.

I guess I never thought about the fact that Jesus' attackers were church people! How did I miss that? I knew their names – the Pharisees and the Sadducees – but it never dawned on me that these were the religious people of their day. These were the church people, and the church people hated Jesus.

During those early days I began meditating on Luke 10 where he says "I am sending you out as a lamb among wolves." There is an eater and eatee in that situation, and it's not the picture I wanted. I wanted to be the eater, but I was being devoured by the church people around me. My vision, dream and calling were being consumed and discarded by the wolves.

And so, to all the young church planters and church planting teams out there: Don't be naive. It's going to be hard. What if neighboring pastors give you a hard time? What if they spread malicious rumors about you? What if other churches turn a cold shoulder to your people, or your vision? You have to be prepared to persevere, push on, keep going forward!

Look, not every church and pastor will be against you – we've had some great partnerships, some great friends, and we've worked together with some great churches to spread the gospel in our community. Just recently I met with some local pastors and they prayed a blessing over our two newest churches! Just don't go into your church plant expecting that. The prevailing mindset of church people toward those who plant churches is not positive. You have to be committed.

You have to keep the 83 Lost Sheep in mind.

It would be easy to get upset at these pastors, or criticize the local church for its lack of support. But something my incredible wife said often in those early days stuck with me:

"We're just accumulating great stories for the future."

God echoed what Julie told me – each of these tests, even though they involved pastors, were things that strengthened my vision for future tests. Without having gone through these situations, my vision may have easily fallen by the wayside. The wolves clarified my vision.

Right now, my biggest critic is another pastor who constantly disparages my church planting.

"Yeah, they're planting churches, but they're doing it all wrong," he says. "They're planting all over the place, and hurting existing churches. They're never going to accomplish anything of value because they don't think through their actions enough. They're not doing it right."

I'm not sure what "right" means. But he is strengthening me.

He says I don't communicate well with other pastors.

He's right, and that's a weakness I'm working on. I need to learn to communicate more effectively. So he's helping me to focus on important weaknesses. I'm learning more and more that critical people can be a blessing.

When I decided I wanted to get engaged to my wife Julie, I was nineteen and she was seventeen. We were children. I look at my kids today (my son Luke just turned seventeen) and I can't believe we were his age. It seems so young!

A guy at our church named Clair Acker came up to me after I announced my engagement.

"Are you crazy?" he asked. "You are so young!"

"I don't know," I said, suddenly confused. "Do you think we're that young?"

"You are SO young! You're teenagers. You're practically kids!"

"Yeah, but when we get married we'll be twenty and eighteen. That's pretty good, isn't it?"

"Sure, it's better, but you'll still be young. You're an idiot. You have no idea what it means to be in love."

His uncertainty put me in a pattern of thinking – *Maybe we are too young,* I thought. *Maybe I haven't considered what it means to be in love.* We were at the Creation Music Festival that year (the largest Christian music festival in the country, held every summer in central PA) and one of the speakers suggested something that got my attention.

"If you think you're in love with someone, choose to be separate for a while. See how that feels. If it feels good, then you ought to stay separate. But if it kills you, if you feel like part of you is missing, if you're dying to talk to them, then maybe you've got something."

That's a great test, I thought to myself at the time.

What brought this up in my mind was Clair – he was the wolf and I was the sheep. He tore up my vision of being married to Julie, but he did it from a place of love. And he helped me, because I had to go back to the Lord of the harvest and ask if I was actually ready.

So Julie and I separated for a short time, shortly before we announced our engagement! We agreed to take one week and not talk at all. No phone calls, no notes, no conversation for a week.

I'll tell you – on Monday I was losing my mind. By Tuesday I thought to myself, *I don't ever want to go this long without talking to her again.* By Wednesday I thought I was going to die if I didn't see her.

I called her on Wednesday.

"This is a bad idea," I said. "I just want to spend some time with you."

She was bawling on the other end of the line.

"I know, I know, I can't take this. I really want to be with you for the rest of my life."

Never again did we question our marriage.

It took that for us to settle the question in our minds that Clair had raised.

I challenged a young couple in our church with the same challenge.

They had been dating since they were fourteen. When they were seventeen and sixteen they came to me and said they wanted to get married as soon as they were old enough.

"Our parents think we're too young, but we're ready."

"I'll tell you what – why don't you do what Julie and I did? Take a week and don't talk to each other. In fact, see if you can go for three weeks."

They agreed.

A few weeks into it I saw the boy at one of our youth events.

"So, Chad, how's it going?"

He looked around, then back at me, his eyes gleaming.

"This is nice! I like this."

"What? That's not what I was expecting you to say."

"Man, I don't have to ask anyone if I want to go to McDonalds for lunch today. If I want to change my major in college next year, I can just change it! No discussions! I like this freedom. I'm not going back."

I saw the girl a few days later.

"How do you feel about this?"

"It's okay," she said. "It's not bad."

They didn't get married. And they're both living wonderful lives, happy to this day that they didn't get married at such a young age.

Someone needed to be 'the wolf' and challenge their vision.

These churches that attacked me, they actually did me a favor because they helped me to figure out what I wanted. I don't want these stories to make anyone feel guilty or angry! I want these folks to know that they helped to clarify my vision, and for that I am so grateful.

I should also say that they Pastor who came to my house with the check, telling us that we should move home, totally apologized, and told me later that he was wrong. I respect that. It takes an amazing courage to admit when we are wrong and seek forgiveness.

I've spent too much time resenting the wolves in my life – I'm realizing now that these wolves are a gift from God, and I need to love them for that. They are not my enemies. This is a new revelation to me. In the same way that Clair helped me by looking me in the eye and saying, "You are an idiot for getting married too early," these critical pastors have helped me better determine the course of my vision.

Clair told me later that he was only trying to challenge me, to make sure I had thought things through. I told him I hadn't really thought things through, at least not until Julie and I took some time apart.

"I know!" he exclaimed, smiling.

I was very young, maybe sixteen years old, when I told my pastor at the time, Omar Beiler, that I thought I was called to be a pastor. We had a guest speaker that Sunday who was challenging people to enter the ministry, and it had resonated with me.

"I'm called to the ministry," I told our pastor after the service. I honestly thought he would hug me and pledge his undying support.

He burst out laughing. Then he looked at me with some confusion.

"You're serious, aren't you?"

"Yes, I am serious!"

I couldn't believe it! *If my own pastor couldn't see it, maybe I am wrong?*

I started praying about it a lot. Just talking to God. And you know what? This got me to the place where I didn't care if the most significant person in my life thought I was crazy – I was going to be a pastor. I had to do this. When that happened, I got strengthened. Instead of his laugh weakening me, I started to realize that it was inspired of God in order to cement my vision. And that he, my pastor, was a true friend.

Who are the wolves in your life? Stop feeling intimidated by them. Stop hating them. Start seeing how they are refining your vision, increasing your courage and providing you with much needed motivation to accomplish what God has called you to do.

It's interesting how God does it. He turns evil attacks into good for us. For these reasons, Romans 8:28 has become a favorite of mine. "All things work together for good", I repeat to myself, "for those who love the Lord, for those who are called according to His purpose".

I hang onto this truth like a life raft.

This concept is often used just slightly off of what it means. "Everything happens for a reason", people often say, as if God orchestrated some evil thing to help us. But that is not our God, and that's not what he said.

What he did promise is that he will make it all work together for good *if we love Him*. So, while He does not orchestrate the evil events (even though they make us grow or help us in some way), he does participate in turning evil events into something good.

Over the years, I have watched helplessly as people I love suffer from all kinds of "wolf" attacks. Some seem to not only survive – they thrive after a horrible event! Others allow a disaster, criticism, or hurt to destroy them completely. The difference is both simple and profound: If you love God, he will turn your evil events into something good. If you don't love him, insist on dealing with it on your own, he sometimes allows you to do that, in whatever way you choose.

Proverbs 24:16 says, "(The Godly) may trip seven times, but each time they will rise again." You may think that the boxer Rocky Balboa would be a surprising source of wisdom, but he said something similar, "It's not how many times you get knocked down. It's how many times you get back up."

Let's put this in perspective: I can't remember failing anything seven times. It's not that I've succeeded at everything I've tried – it's just that usually by the second failure or attack, I conclude that I'll never succeed at that thing. If I last through a third failure, I feel it's confirmed, and I'd consider myself an idiot for even trying again!

Seven attacks. Seven failures. Six more attempts after already failing once. These are the things that legends are made of. If we want to win big, we have to face big wolves, sometimes doing it over and over again. Is it possible that one way God defines evil is not trying again after a failure? And then again after that? And again? And again? God help me get to where I can be defined as a good man, a man that falls seven times but still gets up and keeps trying!

Chapter Six: The Problem With Purses

"Don't take along any money, or a traveler's bag, or even an extra pair of sandals"

Jesus said to his disciples, "Don't take a purse or a bag or sandals." I read that and wondered, *What problem does Jesus have with them being prepared?* For us today that would be like saying don't take your wallet, your briefcase or an extra pair of shoes. So what's his problem with us taking those things with us on our journey?

One angle of this starts with the understanding that entrepreneurs want to be the kind of people who never have to receive anything from anyone. Years ago, one of my church planters voiced what sounded like a worthy goal.

"If I could get by without my church ever having the burden of paying my salary, wouldn't it be nice? What if I was independently wealthy and my church never had to pay me because I had my own money?"

I know of two churches that did this – one guy was a contractor who made his own money, so he never drew a salary. This church never grew past about forty to fifty people. The other church has reached eighty to one hundred people, and the pastor of that church is constantly letting them know that he does not need a salary.

The problem I see here is in regards to vulnerability.

If I'm an entrepreneur and I'm starting a church, and I have no plans of ever collecting a salary, I'm saying one thing to my church:

I don't need you.

Those two churches where the pastor had an outside income never took off, and I think the reason is that by not collecting a salary, they portrayed an attitude that communicated, "I don't need you." But God set up his church to need a pastor, and for the pastor to feel that he needs a congregation. Of course this "needy" relationship can sometimes be warped, but when done right it creates a healthy balance.

We're made to want to give something to people who contribute to us. And when we don't, something happens inside us, a disconnect, a dissonance, that prevents us from connecting. It feels weird. It's not cool.

If I have a student at our school who hasn't managed to pay his school bill, and we allow them to continue in that space of attending for free, they almost always develop bad attitudes. The same thing holds true in counseling: if you are getting counseling and you're not giving something toward your counselor, it's much easier to take it for granted, or even stop going. Very rarely do counselees get real help unless they contribute something substantial to their healing. Maybe you're giving something as simple as friendship, or your trading for your sessions – it doesn't always have to be money, but, if you're not giving something, then too often it's difficult to maintain a good attitude.

I think Jesus was teaching his disciples a valuable lesson – if they entered a relationship (or in this case a home) and showed no vulnerability, it was actually impossible to develop a relationship. So, he was saying, "You guys who are entrepreneurs with self-made-man mentalities – that's strong, and you probably see solutions everywhere, but you have got to start depending on others."

If you don't have any wants or needs, then no one can provide for you, and that's not a good thing. If they can't give you something, then they feel awkward.

I was riding along with someone the other day.

"I'm really hungry," he said.

"Oh," I replied. "I've got a chocolate bar here. You can have it."

"Nah, I'm not going to eat your chocolate bar."

I'll admit, I felt a little offended by that. *Why is my food not good enough for him? Why is my offering not good enough for him?*

I'll tell you why. He didn't want to owe me anything. That's the problem. But we were created to owe each other something, to be in a community that helps one another, depends on each other.

In marriage we owe each other something – at the very least our bodies, according to I Corinthians 7. But also friendship, and emotional support. This give and take, this interdependence, is a healthy thing.

So if a pastor or leader can't allow his people to give to him, then neither will they ever be willing to receive anything of substance from him.

My brother George and I were having this discussion when I first entered the ministry.

"George," I asked, "how do you get to be in full-time ministry? I'm doing ministry, and I'm working hard. But no one is offering me a salary for it. How does that happen?"

"The concept is simple," he said. "But the practice is hard."

"Okay."

"Here's the concept: if you give people what money cannot buy, they'll give you what it can. And they'll gladly give you what it can."

What I learned from George is that my job is to give people the things they can't buy at Wal-Mart: if it's on a shelf at Wal-Mart, then Wal-Mart will provide it. If it's non-tangible, and they desperately need it, then it's my job as a pastor to provide it.

"Help me with this concept," I asked George. "What can people not buy with money?"

"Go to 1 Corinthians 14:1 – 3. See if you can get a hold of that."

I called him back a week later.

"So I've been working on that scripture you gave me. Let me see if I understand this. It says first of all that the Holy Spirit acknowledges there are lots of gifts that come from him but there's one gift the Holy Spirit would like everyone to have."

"You got it," he said. "What is that one?"

"That gift is prophecy. I always thought prophecy was telling the future. Are you telling me this is what the Holy Spirit wants everyone to do, above and beyond everything else?"

"You've got to read the rest of the passage," George said. "It doesn't say prophecy is telling the future. It never mentions telling the future. It says prophecy is strengthening, encouragement and comfort. Those are the things that money cannot buy."

Money cannot purchase emotional and spiritual strength.

Money cannot buy encouragement.

Money cannot buy comfort.

These are currencies of the soul that everybody has to have in order to function, and you can't get it on the shelves at Wal-Mart.

"If you can learn to give those three things," George said, "and you give them in abundance, then people will give back to you. This is why Jesus told his disciples not to take that stuff with them on their journey. If you learn that what you are giving is of such value that people will love giving back to you, you'll never want again."

I was being paid for ministry within months of hearing that wisdom.

Two things happened that brought this into being.

Merrill Smucker came on staff at the church where I was serving. He started out as a full-time volunteer, and had a swagger that helped me so much – he was confident, but not arrogant.

"How are you giving all this time to serve at the church?" I asked him. "How can you afford to do this? And why are you doing it?"

"Oh, that's easy. I'm earning myself a job around here. I'll be hired in a short time."

"Our church doesn't have the money to pay you!" I said. "They're barely paying our senior pastor! How do you think you are going to work your way on to the staff?"

"I don't care. I'm earning it. I'm contributing the kind of stuff that causes people to give more in the offering, to bring their friends to church. This church will grow a lot in the next year or two, and soon they'll be saying that they can't afford to live without me."

He was right – it wasn't long until our church offered him a full-time position.

Shortly after that, our Head Pastor Omar looked me in the eye.

"Here's what I promise you," he said. "I will never go to the board and say 'We have to hire Gerry.' Never. The board will come to me and say that, or it will never be said. If you think you want to serve me, you'll understand soon that you're actually serving the church, and you've got to do it to the point where they say, 'We don't want to live without Gerry – he's going off to work and we're jealous because we'd rather have him working for our church.'"

I ran a floor-cleaning business at the time, working for some local businesses after hours.

"I need my people to come to me," Omar continued, "and say that they hate it when you go to clean floors because then you can't serve them early in the morning and you're not available in the evenings."

I learned it by watching Merrill. It wasn't very long until I had earned my spot, serving the body of Christ until God sent the finances to allow me to do it full time. The church grew, and God moved in the hearts of His people to give me the things money can buy, when I gave them the things it cannot.

George was right.

Most young leaders who want a job serving a church, think that they have to persuade the pastor, or the board, to hire them. They are wrong. What they need to do is serve the people by providing what money cannot buy. God takes it from there.

True encouragement is a rare and beautiful thing. It does not come in a business transaction, nor can it be bought. But when it flows from a genuine heart, it produces an inevitable response. Fake encouragement sounds like flattery. Fake comfort comes off hollow and condescending. False strengthening comes off as criticism and is hurtful.

But a person who waits in the presence of God, not praying for her own happiness or her own ease is a rare thing. If she spends that time sincerely praying for someone else and caring about their life, if she listens to God's heart until she hears what the Father is saying about that other person, then shares with that person what she heard, those things are priceless.

Prophecy is the power of creating with your words. Do it well, and the world conforms to what God instructed you to declare.

Reject self-sufficiency. Set out with only what you need, provide others with the things that money cannot buy, and accept what they have to offer.

Chapter Seven: The Temptation In Distraction

"And don't stop to greet anyone on the road"

Jesus said in verse four, "Do not greet anyone on the road." Seven chapters into this book, and we've only gotten through four verses of Luke ten! This goes to show how much God had to say about leadership and planting churches in this passage.

In Jesus' day, it was considered socially unacceptable not to greet a stranger in your town. You must greet people! And if that stranger needed shelter in your town, every true Hebrew was required to offer them shelter in their own home.

I have a few thoughts on what might have been going through Jesus mind when he told his disciples not to greet people on the road. Remember when Jesus' parents left him in the temple? Jesus was missing for three days! Have you ever lost a kid for three days? Not only would you go crazy with worry, but you might even go to jail for neglect.

But Jesus' parents lost him for three days. How do you do that? How do you misplace the Savior of the world, the Son of God, the Messiah?

I think one possible reason is that they were too culturally concerned. It was the major festival of the year, and they're supposed to greet everyone, be friendly with each person they cross paths with. Maybe Mary and Joseph were so nice they had to say hello to everyone – yet, in all of this socializing, they couldn't keep track of their own children.

Three days into greeting all of these relatives and strangers, pilgrims and worshipers, they suddenly realized something.

They lost Jesus.

I think when Jesus said, "Do not greet anyone on the road," he was saying, "Listen, you've got a job to do, and you have to stay focused on that job."

Ministry has every distraction known to man. The hardest thing about ministry is being disciplined enough to set aside the urgent things in favor of the important. We're all constantly bombarded with things that seem pressing in that moment, but do not have long-term importance. Somehow we have to see past those things and stay focused on the important.

I could spend all day replying to emails that are urgent and completely miss the person in front of me with whom God wants me to talk. I could spend all day attending meetings and answering phone calls, but if these things are handcuffing me from accomplishing important, kingdom activities, then I'm not following Jesus command to "greet no one on the road."

It's all about how we deal with distractions.

If you are one of those social butterflies who has all of the societal stuff down, watch out. Especially if you're a pastor. We pastors naturally want to please everyone! If there is someone who doesn't feel happy with us at the end of the day, then it makes us feel nuts! We all have people trying to impose their needs on us.

I did a funeral once where I could sense a particular family member's anger, directed specifically at me. He was sitting off to my right, glaring a hole right through me. When I said it was time to turn our attention to the life-giving word of God, he snorted out loud and crossed his arms, leaning back in his chair. He was so angry at me and God.

At one point in the funeral service, I mentioned that this person who had died made it very clear that she loved Jesus. We knew she was in heaven.

"Do you all know where you would be if you died today?" I asked.

He lifted his one arm up from where it had been on the chair behind his wife or girlfriend and looked like he was going to walk out. But I had to say this stuff. It was important. Sure, I was having feelings that led me to fear for my own well-being, very urgent feelings in fact. But the over-riding importance of what I had to say could not be held back.

And as I continued to talk, he became less and less hostile. I could see him softening. He started to understand the role the deceased girl had played in our church. I explained that if an unbeliever got to know God, then that person would see the girl again, for eternity.

The service drew to a close.

"If you'd like to take a tiny step today and acknowledge that you'd like to get to know God a little better, would you just raise your eyes and look at me today?"

That man raised his eyes.

In my early days as a pastor, when I was only twenty years old or so, I was fascinated with how many people in the community wanted us, the pastors at our church, to do their weddings. Most of the staff weren't comfortable doing weddings for people who weren't following Christ.

"Wait a minute, guys," I said. "What if there's another answer. Maybe we can offer to do a few sessions of marital counseling with them before we simply shrug them off, just to talk about what it means to be married. What if I could lead these people to Jesus in those three meetings? Then we could do their wedding, right?"

We all agreed that would be fine.

So one of my first couples was Dean and Tracy. They showed up at church one Wednesday night asking if there was a pastor they could talk to about possibly marrying them. I stepped out of the youth group I was leading and went to speak with them.

We walked over to the office, and I conducted my first marital counseling session.

And Dean decided to follow Christ.

First night, first couple.

I was so excited.

"We'll meet a few more times," I told them. "We'll talk about marriage and set a date and I'll do your wedding."

They argued in the parking lot on the way out that night, and Dean jumped on his motorcycle and raced away, roaring down the road.

And Dean was killed in an accident.

Meanwhile, youth group was over and I found Tracy back in the parking lot bawling her eyes out, shaking like a leaf.

I ran over to her.

"What's wrong?"

"Dean just got killed." She could barely speak.

I had just led the guy to Christ less than sixty minutes before. Unbelievable.

This led to my first biker funeral, and the leaders of the gang made it painfully clear that they did not want a church funeral – only a graveside service.

"God let Dean die," they said, anger in their eyes. "We don't want anything to do with a God that would let that happen."

They came in huge groups, their bikes rumbling up the road, and all of them wore the same motorcycle jackets. Many of their jackets had filthy language and curses on the patches. This was my first funeral, my first experience leading a service at graveside.

"I want you all to know," I said at one point, "that Dean will be in heaven, and I'll get to see him again. Because Dean accepted Christ as his savior two nights ago. The Bible tells me that means I'm going to see him again for eternity."

They glared at me from under their bandanas, the leather reflecting the sunshine.

"I want to know," I continued, "how many of you can say that?"

That group became so hostile I thought they were going to shove me into the grave. Literally, some of the Christians who were there had to gather around me to keep them from pushing me in. It was rough, and I was a scared young preacher.

But for me, in those two instances, it was a focus issue.

You have to stay so focused on the end goal that nothing can distract you: not society, not church-world, not family. Not fear.

In my second or third year at our church plant in Gettysburg, I was still hurting a lot from what had happened at my home church, how I had been sent out, things I couldn't talk to anyone about it. I really couldn't function in that area of my life at the time.

My brother George called me from Tampa.

"Gerry, there is a revival service happening down here with a guy from Australia, Rodney Howard Brown. You ever hear of him?"

"No, never heard of him."

"There's something unique going on down here at his church meetings in Lakeland. You've got to get down here."

"I'm not coming – there are way too many things for me to be doing here at church."

To be honest, I was so suspicious of church at that point. I thought most church people were hypocrites and judgmental. Looking back, I really wonder how I could pastor at that point, or how God could use me. I just don't know.

"I know where you're at," George said. "I know how bitter you are. But you need to come. This would be really good for you. I went to this thing and got so much healing the first night."

"I did notice a change in you," I said, hesitantly.

"You have to come. This is the second week of consecutive nightly services. You're coming week after next."

"I've got stuff planned."

"Too bad. I've sent you plane tickets already. You're coming."

This was the closest George ever got to giving me an order (except for earlier in my life when he told me never to come to him with a problem before asking God about it).

"Fine," I grumbled. "I'll come to your stupid services."

So I went. And God met me so big there that I cried for three days straight about my pain, my judgmental heart, about how God called me back to the ministry. I cried and cried and cried.

During the last evening I was there, the place was packed. This was supposed to be the first church building in America that seated 10,000 people and it was packed. I had finally arrived early enough on that particular night that I had a seat on the center aisle, right on the end. I worked hard that night to get a good seat, and I was so excited about what God had done in my heart.

Suddenly I saw him: Pastor Carl Strader. During a worship song, he left the platform and walked down the middle aisle. I noticed that when he came by me, he was not looking at anyone – his eyes were on the floor. As he got closer, I started getting more and more excited.

This was the guy who led the services that completely changed my heart – this was the man who was responsible for helping me work through so much in those last few days. *If he so much as looks at me*, I thought to myself, *I'll step out in the aisle and hug him.*

He went right by me, within six inches, and I never moved, because he didn't so much as raise his eyes.

I asked the Holy Spirit, *Why is this moment capturing my attention the way it is?*

Then I realized: if Carl Strader hadn't been so focused on that important task, if he would have done the socially "nice" thing and made eye contact with people as he walked back the aisle, he would have been mobbed by those like me wanting to thank him. He knew that if he started hugging people, the entire service would have stopped for him to continue greeting people. If, just once, he would have looked at one person, he would have lost the meeting.

He understood focus.

Is our desire for accolades impeding our focus? Is the social pressure to be nice to everyone clouding our vision?

Jesus was telling his disciples that when he sent them on the road to deliver a message, their job was to get the message out. If they couldn't get that, they couldn't lead.

Five years ago a man came to me at our church.

"I want to do what you've said you never have enough time to do – visitation," he said. "I love visiting people in hospitals, I love praying for people in that environment."

"This is gold," I said. "You are going to be my new visitation pastor."

So one day we got a call in the office from a family new to our church.

"You've never met my mom," the lady said, "but she's at Hershey Medical Center right now and she's probably not going to make it through the night. We really need someone up there – she's asking to see a pastor. She wants someone to pray with her. Can you please visit her? It would mean the world to us."

"Absolutely," I said. "But I'm in Tampa and I can't make it there. We will get someone from the church there tonight."

So I called my new visitation pastor. We'll call him Paul.

"Paul? You still want to be my visitation pastor? This is really important. I need you to get to Hershey Medical Center to see this lady. She's not going to make it very long. Tell her you were sent by me to visit. Give her my love. And give her an opportunity to meet Christ."

"No problem," he said. "Got it."

The next day I called Paul.

"Hey, Paul, how'd it go last night?"

"Oh, no."

"What?"

"I forgot."

"You forgot?" I couldn't believe it. My heart sank. "Paul, I told you the person was dying and they wanted to see a pastor! What do you mean you forgot?"

"When I got to Hershey Medical Center, my friend was in the lobby and I hadn't seen this friend for such a long time. We had parted on bad terms, and we got talking. Hours later, I left, and I totally forgot to visit that woman."

So I called one of the family friends.

"Have you heard anything about the lady at Hershey Medical Center?" I asked urgently.

"Yeah," they said. "She died last night."

So we had a brand new family feeling let down by the church – I had given them my word. And more importantly, someone died, wanting to meet God, and who knows if they had been able to. All because he forgot!

I called Paul back.

"Paul, I don't care how gifted you are. I don't care! You could have been a horse and done a better job yesterday! You let me down, man. We now have no idea where this lady is spending eternity. Your job was to find that out. I cannot believe you forgot. You forgot! You can talk to your friend all day, but if you don't do what you're sent to do first, you can't be my visitation pastor."

This is precisely what Jesus was saying.

If you don't focus, people will miss out on encountering God.

It doesn't get much more important than that.

Chapter Eight: It's About Blessing, Stupid

"Whenever you enter a home, give it your blessing"

Jesus said whenever you enter a house, say peace to that house. I think the meaning can be interpreted a little broader: when you first engage in a relationship, make sure you start that relationship off well. If you want to be influential, it has to start with blessing.

Blessing literally means " to compliment."

Imagine this: I come into your house and the first thing I say is some kind of criticism.

"This place is a dump."

"Why would you move your family here?"

"This is the dumbest place to live."

"I hate what you've done to the place".

"What were you thinking when you bought a sofa that color?"

How would you feel about me?

Let's assume we don't have a relationship where we can kid around with each other. If you took me seriously, you would want to kick me out, literally.

So how do we think the world can hear us when all they get from us is criticism? Sometimes I think all the world hears from the church are things like:

"If you're gay, you're stupid and going to hell."

"You're an idiot if you drink any alcohol, ever."

"Only uneducated people smoke."

"If you're pro-choice, you are a hateful person."

"If you're a democrat, then you're at least misguided, and maybe not even a Christian."

Jesus said, "When you enter a house, first say 'peace to this house'." He was saying that every relationship should start with a blessing. A compliment.

How hard is this?

It shouldn't be hard at all.

This is why so many mothers-in-law are despised by their sons-in-law, because they start off the relationship saying (either out loud or by demonstration) "You're not good enough for my daughter" and "You can't do anything right."

I heard a joke recently that behind every good man is a surprised mother-in-law.

Now I do have to say, I love my mother-in-law. Julie jokes that she gets annoyed because her mother likes me better than her. My mother-in-law, Janice Phipps, loved me in spite of all the stuff I did, as I put her daughter at risk again and again with all my crazy schemes. So I've never felt that my mother-in-law thinks I'm not good enough for her daughter.

But I know a lot of guys who do. They despise their mother-in-laws because they're so full of criticism. Their mother-in-laws never bless them.

When my oldest daughter was six months old we were at a family gathering. Someone suggested we go around the circle and play the blessing game.

We kind of rolled our eyes.

"What the heck is the blessing game?" someone asked.

"It's a compliment. Just say something nice to the person on your right. How hard is that?"

How could we argue? Everyone kind of grumbled and sighed but in the end someone said, "Okay, we'll give it a shot."

"I'll start," my aunt said. "Dave, you're one of the smartest business men I've ever met."

Dave turned to his right.

"Mark, I've always admired the way you think through issues."

I'm sitting to the left of my cousin who started the game, so I would go last. To my left, the person who would have to "bless" me, was my mother-in-law.

In those days I wasn't thinking very positively about myself. Candace was a baby, I wasn't making a decent living and my in-laws were helping us out a lot. They had helped me pay for college, and I was still in college at that point. I was thinking that my mother-in-law was going to have to work pretty hard to get beyond the negatives that she felt about me. *What would she say? How would she bless me?*

I was sweating bullets.

Should I run to the bathroom?

Could the roof please cave in?

A thousand examples of stupid things I did rushed into my head. I remembered how they had to gently coach me to leave their house at a decent hour when Julie and I were dating.

I remembered how I lost my driver's license for ten years as a young man. She and my father-in-law had so patiently driven me everywhere without complaining.

I remembered the day that little Candace fell off our bed after I laid her down for a nap. She had never rolled over before, but that day she rolled off onto the floor. I felt like a horrible father.

When that group got around to her, she could have made a joke. Or jokes. If she started recounting the stupid things I had done in the past, she could go on all day! My selfish little mind raced with crazy memories of mistakes and foolish things I had done, as that blessing game wound toward our side of the room.

What would she say?

Finally it came to her. I was holding six-month old Candace on my lap.

"Gerry," she says quietly, "I think you might be the best father that I've ever seen."

I just started crying. I can't even tell the story without getting emotional. That's how much it meant to me, and I fell in love with her on the spot. To this day I would do anything for her, because this is how she treats me.

Want to know why most parents can't influence their teenagers?

They criticize their kids' music.

They criticize their kids' clothes.

They criticize their kids' friends.

They criticize their kids' choice of career.

They criticize EVERYTHING about their kid! And then they wonder why they have no influence.

Pastors want to know why no one comes to their church.

Often it's because in subtle ways, and in big ways, they put people down. No one wants to hang around that – it doesn't matter how good of a speaker you are. The bottom line? People will not go to a place that makes them hate themselves. They're not coming back.

I'm not saying that preachers have to water down their messages – even fire and brimstone preachers can be good at it, if they help the listener feel redeemable. But being an endless critic will get you nowhere. This is precisely why we're not influencing our world today. The first thing the world thinks about when they hear "Christian" is the list of things they think we're against:

Swearing.

Homosexuality.

Abortion.

Liberalism.

Alcohol.

Smoking.

Fun.

Until the world feels complimented and blessed by us, we will never have influence.

When I first started hanging out with Merrill Smucker, before I was on staff at Victory Chapel, I remember driving around with him one day. We pulled into a gas station, and I went inside while he started pumping gas. I picked out a soda, bought it and left.

The person behind the counter and I didn't even make eye contact.

Five minutes later, Merrill goes into the store to pay for the gas. I decided to go back in and get a pack of gum. There are three people working there – one person behind the deli counter and two behind the cash registers – and as I'm looking around for gum, I can hear Merrill bantering back and forth with all three of them.

"Well, don't you look nice today!" he said to one of them.

"Thank you, sir, that's so nice of you!"

As Merrill paid, he talked with the cashier.

"You're quick at counting out change. Wow."

The cashier didn't say anything, but she smiled to herself.

He had something nice to say to each person in that store, even though he didn't know any of them, and, from the time he entered to the time he left, their faces went from neutral expressions to happy ones.

So anyway, he checked out and walked to the car.

I paid for my gum.

"Who is that guy?" the lady behind the register asked.

"I came with him," I said.

"I thought you did. Who is he?"

"That's Pastor Merrill Smucker from Victory Chapel."

"That must be a great church," she said, shaking her head in disbelief that a pastor would be so nice to her.

"Yeah, it is," I said. "You should come visit sometime."

But inside I was thinking, *I was just in here three minutes ago and these people didn't even recognize me! How is that? I just bought a soda and they didn't care who I was. The only reason she spoke to me was to find out who Merrill was.*

Why did they want to know who Merrill was?

That's easy: before he left the store he had complimented every single worker in there. And because of that, they wanted to know his name. They wanted to know who he was. The Holy Spirit really started getting on my case about this, so when I got back out to the car, I brought it up with Merrill.

"That person wanted to know who you were," I said.

"Yeah, well," he said, just kind of shrugging it off. "I love when I'm like this. I love when I have something nice to say to everyone. Don't you just love it when you're like that?"

I was at a loss.

"I can't remember that I've ever really done that in my life."

That day I made myself a commitment: I was going to become like Merrill Smucker. I was going to be someone that, when I left a room, people would want to know who I was because I made them feel accepted and loved.

Jesus must have been like that.

When I was fourteen, my cousin Anthony Beiler went on a missions trip to Central America. And he never came back. He went swimming one day and drowned. They found him a day or two later and shipped him home. I couldn't go to the funeral because I was so broken up by it. His dad even called me.

"Did you know you were Tony's best friend in the world?"

"Oh, I don't think so," I mumbled

"You were."

I just couldn't understand how that was possible.

"If you died today," he asked me, "who would you see as your best friend?"

"I don't know," I said.

I started thinking. I couldn't think of any close friends. None.

"Why don't I have any close friends?" I asked myself.

So I asked God to teach me how to have friends, and the Holy Spirit started showing me people who were good at having friends.

Mel Beiler was one of these guys that I started watching.

At first I thought he didn't know anything. All he did was say nice things about people. But I decided to give it a try, this whole idea of blessing people. It was difficult! I discovered that being nice did not come naturally to me, and I found it hard to think up encouraging things to say to people. I started to realize that I didn't have friends because I was usually critical and angry.

That's when I started on this quest for friendship.

And this led up to my time with Merrill Smucker.

Why is Merrill so popular? I wondered. The more I hung out with him, the more I realized that there wasn't one person in southern Lancaster County who didn't know this guy's name. Almost every time he left a room, people were asking, "Who is that guy? I have to know him."

Jesus says that when you walk into somebody's house, make sure there's a blessing in it. Years ago I was trying to work on this. I was the youth pastor at Victory Chapel and a mother came to me.

"Pastor Gerry, would you pray for me?"

"Sure. Why?"

"My two teenage boys hate me."

"That's impossible! Boys don't hate their mothers! What are you talking about?"

"They do. I need prayer."

I was kind of shocked.

"I don't know what to say. I'm not a counselor. But I can definitely pray with you."

The next day she brought her two boys to church and came into the office.

"Where are the boys?" I asked.

"They're outside, playing."

"Okay, well, why don't you bring the boys in here?"

So we went outside and brought them in.

"Boys, I'm not sure if I should be saying this, but your mom says you hate her? I can't imagine that's true."

"Yeah, pretty much," they both agreed.

I was stunned.

"How can you hate your mother? She gave birth to you. She's been serving you all these years."

One of the boys looked back at me with an empty look in his eyes.

"I don't know. I guess because she hates us."

I turned to the mother.

"You don't hate your boys, do you?"

She nodded.

My eyes opened up wide and I took a deep breath, but she started talking.

"They are hateful young men," she complained. "You don't understand our house. It is not a pleasant place to be – these two are hateful people!"

What do you say to that?

"Let's pray," I said. I didn't know what else to do. But when nothing else works, we believers have a trump card!

As we were praying, something came into my mind. The Bible says we love him because he first loved us. Those two boys hated their mother because their mother first hated them. It worked both ways.

"Okay, boys, you can go outside to play."

We watched as they walked out, and the door closed slowly behind them.

"I'll tell you what," I said. "Here's a tablet and a pen. Could you write down ten things you like about your boys? Just ten. I know you have all those things you hate, because you've already listed out how they're mean and nasty and hateful and dirty and you hate their hair. Give me ten things you like."

She took the tablet.

"I'm going to step out for a minute," I said. "I'll be right back."

When I came back, I looked at her tablet.

Nothing.

"Honestly? Nothing? Nothing that you like about your boys?"

She shook her head.

"There isn't one thing I like about them. In fact, there's not one thing about those boys that I can stand."

"Well, I think I'm starting to get the picture here. I could name you ten things about your boys that I like, and I just met them."

"Go ahead."

"Great, give me the tablet."

She handed it to me.

"I think their hair is sort of cool and gutsy. They are hilarious – they're always cracking jokes."

"But they're mean jokes," she said.

"They're funny! Give them that. They're also very athletic, and they're tall."

"Yeah, they eat like hogs," she grumbled.

I went on and listed ten things.

"So here's the deal," I said. "This is what the Holy Spirit gave to me. I want you to go home and everyday I want you to take one thing on my list and just say it over your boys."

"It'll be awkward," she protested.

"I don't care! Find a place to say this over your boys. One compliment each day. Your boys hate you because you hate them."

Eventually our conversation came to an end. She folded up the paper and left.

The next day she called me.

"I told them that sometimes they're nice."

"How'd they act?" I asked.

"They just swore at me and went out to play like they always do."

"Okay, let's see what happens tomorrow."

The next day she called me again.

"We had a good day. A really good day."

"I didn't expect it to work that fast," I said. "Tell me about it."

"Today I told them that I really appreciated it when they took out the garbage without complaining."

"That's a pretty big step," I said. "Way to go."

"Yeah, it is!"

The next day she called me again. This was the third day.

"We've had two good days in a row. I haven't had two good days with my boys since, I don't know, maybe never."

"Well, let's see how today goes. What are you going to tell them?"

"I already told them. This morning I thought of an extra one, so I told them two today. Two things I like about them."

"So how is your day going so far?"

"Fantastic! I get this. I'm not going to call you anymore. From now on I will always say nice things about my boys."

Before we had met up, her oldest boy had run away from home repeatedly and swore at her all the time. He behaved terribly. But after she started blessing him, he never ran away again. The second boy became one of the most lovely little boys, kind and generous and loving.

"What do you think happened?" I asked one day.

"They're just reflecting back what I am," she said, grinning so big, and nearly crying.

This is such a huge leadership principle. Jesus opened up his ministry with "blessed are the poor in spirit," "blessed are the meek," "blessed are those that mourn." I don't think these were blessings the way that we view blessings, as holy incantations. I don't think it was a "thou art blessed thou blessable person."

Jesus was saying, if you're going through a tough time in life and you're mourning, the cool thing is that life is not all sad — you might be crying today, but the next thing you know, you'll be happy again. You're at the bottom and it's all going to get better from there. He encouraged people, especially those who found themselves in the margins of society.

One of the gospels say that Jesus went to the other side of the lake on a boat, and the next morning the people he had been speaking with were at the other side waiting for him. They walked around the entire lake, probably spending the entire night hiking to catch up with Jesus! Why?

Because they never had anyone compliment them like that before. No one had ever blessed them, even in their times of weakness.

A young lady, who I will call Millie, probably in her twenties, joined us on a recent trip to Nepal. At one point, once we were over there, I lined up the team and asked them to introduce themselves to a group of Nepalese pastors.

Everyone came up, and they were all terrified, but none more so than Millie.

"Don't make me speak in public, Gerry," she begged.

"I'm not going to make you speak. Just introduce yourself. Just say hi."

This is the girl we had to coax into the van just to get her out of the country. She had signed up for the trip, but then on the day we were supposed to leave, she became terrified. Finally we had convinced her to come.

And there we were, standing up in front of a group.

"Just your name, Millie, you can do it."

She nodded but she looked horrified.

So we went down the line, and everyone said their name and where they were from.

Then it was Millie's turn.

"Hi, I'm Millie," she said. But just as the next person was about to introduce themselves, she suddenly interrupted them and kept speaking!

"Not too long ago I came to Freedom Valley for the first time. And the reason I'm still going to Freedom Valley is that I have never been blessed or complimented before in my life. I can't remember one person ever saying one kind thing to me."

By now she was crying her eyes out, but she just kept talking. All of us were crying, too, as were all the Nepalese pastors gathered there.

"I can never come to Gerry's church without somebody saying something kind and sweet to me. I had been told to watch out for this church, because they were a cult, or at least weird. By the third time I was there, I said I didn't even care what they were selling – if you want me to get to know Jesus, then that's what I'll do, because I've never been treated like this before. I just want you pastors to know how wonderful it is to be around people who love you and choose to say nice things to you."

Everyone inside that Nepalese church was crying at this point. Talking through an interpreter makes it very difficult to convey emotion, but this crowd felt her gentle spirit. And everyone knew what she was talking about. We've all been there. We've all been rejected, labeled as not good enough, called misfits. All of us. Sometimes by others, but many times the rejection comes from within.

I remember when my youth leader Galen Smoker was teaching us about spiritual gifts in the hay loft of a horse barn at Camp Hebron. I had never heard of spiritual gifts before.

"Everybody has a spiritual gift," Galen said. "Just read 1 Corinthians 12: he gives spiritual gifts to everyone."

I was sitting in that youth group, and I was thinking to myself, *I don't think so. I don't have any gifts. You just named them all and none of them sounded like anything that I have.*

Galen continued, as if he could read my mind.

"I'll tell you what, sometimes they're hard to see in yourself, so let's take a moment and turn to the person closest to you and talk through the gifts and help each other discover what each of your gifts are."

Sitting next to me was Carl Smucker. I was not friends with Carl at that point because I had a little crush on this girl named Fan. Carl could sing and play the piano and I could see that Fan was not opposed to his attention. I was jealous of him in every way: he was talented with obvious spiritual gifts, and he was getting the girl I was at least a little bit interested in.

I froze because I didn't want to say anything nice to Carl. I was a competitive kid and it seemed like he was everything I wanted to be. He could sing, had a sense of humor, was successful and I was fairly certain he was better looking than me.

But Carl beat me to it.

"Gerry," he said, "you have the clearest gift of teaching I've ever seen in my life."

What?

"Carl, how the heck can you say that?"

He pointed to the paper that Galen gave us.

"It says here that a love of understanding how information works in people's lives and how it changes people is an indicator of a teaching gift. And you're constantly trying to understand little details and concepts that not everyone cares about. Then, when you figure it out, you want to share it with people. That's a teaching gift."

I let those words sink in.

"Maybe. Maybe I do. Maybe I've got a teaching gift."

Wow.

I don't remember what I said back to him. All that I remember was that Carl, this guy I wasn't too crazy about, blessed me. He helped me discover my spiritual gift. From that moment forward I didn't care how much more talented he was than me because he had blessed me.

Do you know that Paul says in Galatians that Peter, James and John saw the gifts in him? Paul was this murderous, angry heathen, but those three saw his gifts. There seems to be some connection between Paul's leadership and the fact that the big three saw gifts in him.

Think about that.

What if we complimented the biggest critics in our world? What if we told politicians from camps we disagree with that we appreciate how much they care about the people they are representing? How much influence would we have if we started talking to our world that way?

Don't curse the house. Bless the house.

When we first started Freedom Valley, I was praying about one of the pastors who was very critical of me.

"God, what should I do about this guy?"

Bless him.

"Bless him? What do you mean?"

God pointed something out to me, not in an audible voice, but in my spirit: *That critical pastor just announced that he started a building project but he has no money. Why don't you give him yours?*

"But God, we've got $5,000 in our building fund. That's it! People gave this for our building – I can't give their money away. It's actually unethical. The IRS could put me in jail for this."

Not if you get their permission.

So at the next board meeting I brought it up.

"I feel like God is telling me to bless this church that has been criticizing us a lot."

"What do you have in mind, pastor?" one of the board members asked. "You want us all to say something nice about them right now?"

"No. In this case I think we should bless them financially."

No one said a word.

"I'd like to take our entire building fund and give it to them," I continued.

The tension in the room spiked.

"You can't take my money and give it away," one guy said. "That's my money I put in there for our church."

"Well," I asked, "is it your money or did you give it to God? What if that church stopped saying all that negative stuff? What if they started telling folks that we are on their team, that our main concern is God's kingdom?"

"But what if we give the money and nothing good happens?"

"C'mon, guys. They're a church. God's going to use the money for his glory, no matter what the outcome."

By the end of the meeting, I got the agreement.

The next day I walked over to that church with a $5,000 check in my hand.

"Pastor, can I talk to you?"

"Sure," he said, a little surprised to see me there. "What's up?"

"I felt like God told me to bless you because our church is more about the success of your church than the success of our church. That's the way we need to be. And scripture says I should think of you more highly than myself. If I think of you more highly, then I ought to give you my money. I know you're in a building project, and we don't have a building coming for a while. We were going to save up the money but I feel that you need this money more than us."

"Thank you. That's really nice of you," he said, taking the check and looking at it. I think he was expecting it to be $100 or something.

He looked back at me with tears in his eyes.

"Gerry, this is $5,000!"

"I know."

"Why would you do this?"

"We are on the same team," I said. "You're leading a great church here. You prayed our church into existence, and I should honor you for that."

"This is staggering," he said.

I never remember hearing another word of criticism coming from anyone who attended that church.

Chapter Nine: The Magic Pronoun Principle

"Eat whatever is set before you"

I was in the sanctuary the other week, moving chairs, and someone entered the room.

"Pastor Gerry, can I help?"

I would have preferred to do it on my own – it sounds heartless, but I had a feeling that if this particular person helped me with the chairs, it would take five times as long.

Inside I was groaning, thinking, "I got this covered!" But in the next moment I realized I had to let him help.

Omar (my mentor) called it the Magic Pronoun Principle.

"If someone attends our church for six months," he said, "and you talk to them about the church, they might call it 'Omar's church' or 'the church I got invited to.' In other words, it's a third person, it's someone else's deal. But watch this magically happen: the first time you ask that same person to help you move chairs or set up tables or serve in nursery, from that day forward they'll talk about 'my church.'"

It's true.

If you can let people help or give to you, then you have the dedication of their hearts.

This is counter-intuitive – you would think that by feeding them, by serving them, you would make them feel part of the church. But it's the opposite. It's only by allowing people to serve the church, instead of having the church serve them, that they begin to feel part of the body.

Being fed is not about being fed. Being fed is actually more about feeding.

My wife always says that mostly people just want to be heard. For most people to feel heard, they need to give something or contribute something. Otherwise they'll never feel like they have a voice.

Jeff Deitrich at our South Hanover congregation decided to put an interesting advertisement in his community.

"We're going to do work projects in the neighborhood. Everybody tell your friends that we'll come to your house and do anything you want."

I called the newspaper and told them I had a news piece they might be interested in. The reporters I knew got right back to me.

"Yes, we are very interested!"

They took pictures of Jeff mowing someone's lawn and put it on the front page of the paper. A front page article!

"Local Church Will Do Free Projects For Anyone".

Jeff got six calls that week from people in the community, not from people who wanted his help doing projects at their own homes, but from folks who wanted to help. They're not even part of the church. They're not even Christians. But there is this basic need inside people: they want to help other people.

A few of those folks ended up coming to church.

Why?

"Well, you let us help," they said. "The least we can do is show up in church."

When you let people get involved, a connection forms.

A friend of mine who is a pastor made an observation.

"Isn't it interesting that it would appear the disciples weren't saved yet when they helped Jesus pass out the fishes and loaves for the feeding of the 5000? They hadn't confessed Jesus as Lord yet." Yet all of those acts of service weren't making them grumpy. They didn't complain about being overworked. Serving actually drew them closer to Jesus.

In one of the gospels it doesn't even look like he had recruited them to be his disciples yet. They were just tagging along to help out. This is huge – before salvation, Jesus was getting people involved in service. As our church started grasping this concept, I thought of an idea.

"Let's start advertising for musicians for our worship team."

Not everyone agreed.

"But they've got to be Christians," some people said. "They're ministering – we've got to be sure that . . ."

"Ahhh, maybe not," I said. "Here's what I'm sure of: if someone hangs out with our worship leader for any amount of time, Mark's going to lead them to Christ sooner or later. He's always asking people, 'Do you know Jesus?' Wouldn't it be ideal if Mark had three musicians who aren't Christians?"

"Oh, I don't know," Mark said.

"C'mon, Mark! Have a little confidence. You are somebody who loves Jesus! They're going to get to meet Jesus through you!"

"Yeah, but, every worship seminar you go to says that you have to carefully screen these people and make sure their character is right. I wouldn't have any of that if we just started taking whoever showed up and could play an instrument."

"Mark, what do we have to do for you to have a drummer or a bass player that isn't a Christian? Wouldn't this be the ideal situation?"

I went through this whole conversation with him.

Finally, he started to cave. And for a while, Mark became one of our chief salvation guys because he invited these folks from outside of church to come play music.

Our affiliate church in Red Lion, Pennsylvania, advertised by putting it on their front sign. Another church put an advertisement on Craig's List:

"Musicians wanted."

"Do we have to come from within your church?" potential musicians would ask.

"No."

"Well, we don't know if we believe what you believe."

"It doesn't matter. If you want to come play, come on."

This is still questionable in the church world. I'm not even sure it's a great thing unless you have a worship leader who is really connected to Jesus and has their stuff together.

But Jesus said "Eat what is set before you." He is saying you've got to let people give, you've got to let people serve in some way. If you can't receive something that they have worked on or are talented at, you can't receive their hearts.

Back when I was a youth leader we went on a trip to Mexico. I always tried to take unsaved kids along, and many of them decided to follow Jesus on these trips. This posed certain problems though – at one point a group of girls that came with me to Mexico actually smuggled booze with them! On a church trip!

"Will you at least promise to listen to me?" I asked. "I can't have you sneaking off and getting into dangerous situations."

They promised they wouldn't get into trouble.

On one of these trips we went to Tampico. Clair Acker, our friend and missionary, had us building something on an island out in a lake. There were refugees living on that island, fleeing north and away from the war, and they were flooding Tampico.

"Every morning you'll need to get this bus, to that taxi, to this boat," Clair told us. There were two buses, and I had twenty-one kids to get through this gauntlet, so I couldn't be with all of them. My leaders were going nuts with worry.

Finally, when we got to the canoes that went across to the island, we had to carry bags of cement on the boats. Then, after arriving at shore, we had to take turns carrying these bags of cement to the location, about a mile away.

"We're building the very first building in town," Clair said. "There are no other real buildings."

"What do you mean there are no other buildings?"

"It's a squatters town. They're not served with postal service or medicine – there's nothing! They don't have the materials, and even if they did they'd have no idea what to do. So we're building the first building."

We almost carried that entire structure into town on our backs.

We set up teams of four to carry a sack of concrete because you had to keep switching every hundred feet or so. They weighed 80 pounds, and those were high school kids carrying that stuff. By the time we got there, everyone was dead tired.

But this little town was so excited to see us. They couldn't wait to have a real building. Next to the location for the building was a lady living in a hollowed-out tree with her granddaughters. The parents had been killed in the war. All she had was this hollowed-out tree where she kept some things, and she slept around the base of the tree.

She was so excited that we were there.

We were building a church building, and this church was also going to be the post office and the medical center and perhaps a school. On the first day, we started carrying this stuff in and we were digging holes and putting concrete in the holes around the posts. This lady from the hollowed-out tree came over and started talking to Clair in Spanish. So I walked over to them.

"What's she saying?" I asked him.

"She wants to make us lunch, and she wants to know who is in charge. So I told her you're in charge, because you're the guest pastor and I told her I would ask you if she could make you lunch."

"That's so nice," I said, looking at her, hoping she could understand the meaning of my gestures and facial expressions. "Thank you so much."

97

Clair was kind of behind the lady from where I was standing, and when she turned toward me, he was making motions behind her that clearly said, "Don't do it!"

"Such a bad idea," Clair said as the interpreter and the lady walked away.

"Why? What's wrong?"

"First of all, she doesn't have anything sanitary. She doesn't own anything. Secondly, do you see a chicken? Just watch."

So we went back to work.

"Clair, you worry too much. Doesn't the Bible say, "Eat what is set before you'?"

"Okay, I warned you," he said. "It's on you now."

Then I hear a couple of my kids shouting to each other.

"Hey, look at that funny lady! She's chasing a bird down the road!"

That's not a bird, I thought. *That's a chicken: the scrawniest chicken I had ever seen.*

She chased the chicken down the road with a machete, grabbed it, and with one quick motion cut the head off.

"Ewww, what is she doing?" the same kids exclaimed. "What's going on?"

She threw it on to the ground, and it jumped around for a while without a head, blood spurting into the dirt. My kids started throwing up all over the place.

"What is she doing?" they exclaimed, still in shock.

"I'll tell you what she's doing," I said. "She's making our lunch."

"We are not eating that!" they yelled. "You cannot make us eat that!"

So I gathered everyone together.

"Look, the Bible says we should eat what is set before us. It's one of the ways that we accept people. Can you let her do this?"

Some of the kids flat out said, "No way."

"Okay," I said. "But I'm going to eat it. And if she offers me seconds, I'm going to do my best. Besides, what is so bad about this? Haven't you ever seen a chicken get butchered before?"

"No way," one of the kids said, wiping vomit from his mouth. "I thought chicken came from the grocery store. I'd never eat chicken that was butchered like that."

So she feathered the chicken, then she chopped it. Bones and all went into the big pot of rice. We did our best and we ate what we could. Eating a chicken and spitting out the bones is a foreign experience.

That night, before we went back to where we were staying, we held our first service in the outline of the building. And the "chicken lady" who lived out of a hollowed tree was the first person to come to the front and decide to follow Jesus.

But I could have said anything that night and she would have responded. When we ate her food, we accepted her as a person.

This is key.

Pastors today, myself included, are really tempted to say, "No, no, no, that's okay. I don't need your help. I've got it." But we're undoing the laborers thing. We're not letting people become laborers because we're too self-sufficient, even too efficient. This is an acceptance thing – I have to accept what you offer me in order for you to feel "in".

Then the pronoun changes, from "theirs" to "ours".

Chapter Ten: Quid Pro Quo

"Those who work deserve their pay..."

Marvin came into my office one day and I had the same conversation with him that Omar had with me all those years before.

"I want to be in full-time ministry," he said to me, "and you're the one who persuaded me to go off to Bible college, so now what? You told me that part, what's the next part?"

"Marvin, I want you on my staff, I'll be honest with you," I said. "The second thing I'm going to be real honest about is that I'm never going to mention that out loud to anyone else but you, and this is the last time you'll hear it. If my people don't come to me and say, we have got to hire Marvin, then it probably isn't going to happen."

"You're not getting a purse or bag or sandals," I said. "You're going to have to earn your spot."

"What?" he asked. I think he was a little disappointed.

"I'll tell you where to start. Move to New Oxford with us. Just start serving our church, and see what happens. I'll get the process started."

At the next board meeting, I made the announcement.

"There's a young man who wants to come here and serve us. He's a good guy, someone I've worked with for a long time. I know him well. You can trust him. He's single, and he says he doesn't need any money. He's just going to serve in the church."

I told them a little more about Marvin.

"One thing he needs is a place to stay. I'm going to pass around a tablet – if you're willing for him to stay at your house for a short period of time, perhaps a month, put your name on the tablet and we'll move him from house to house to house. You're signing up for one month: this includes feeding him and providing a place to sleep."

The first people on the list were Dave and Dana Creel.

"We'd love to have him," they said. "Here's the thing: we're going to travel this summer and could use someone to mow the grass and someone to feed the cat and make sure the house looks lived in. This is perfect for us – let Marvin come live in our house for a month."

So Marvin moved in with them in June. About three weeks into it, the Creels came to a board meeting.

"Our house has never looked this good, ever! We've been home from our trip for a week and he makes food, cooks, mows the grass, and offered to wash my car the other day. He even vacuums! His room is clean. There is no reason that he couldn't stay another month, if he wants to."

The second couple on the list spoke up.

"Hey, hold on! We want to have him. We've got little kids, and a yard that needs mowed, and having someone around to help out sounds great to us."

"I already told Dave and Dana they could have him for another month, but you can definitely have him after that."

So at the next month's board meeting, someone asked about Marvin.

"Marvin can stay with us for the rest of his life, if he wants," Dave and Dana were saying. "He's in."

"Why?" I asked.

"Look, we needed counseling and he was there for us. He taught us some spiritual principles we didn't know before. He mows the grass. He vacuums the house. He helps with the dishes. He's a wonderful guy to have in the house. We want to keep him!"

The other couple nearly jumped out of their seats.

"That's not fair!"

"Wait a minute!" I said. "Not too long ago, you guys said you could keep him maybe a month. Now you're fighting over him?"

"Yeah, we're fighting over him!" they said, and we all laughed.

Marvin never made it down the list past the second house. After staying with the first couple for months, the second couple finally persuaded him that it's not fair for him to stay with the same family all the time, so he went to their house. They kept him until he had enough salary to get his own apartment.

Six months into his move to New Oxford to work at our church on a volunteer basis, he was doing anything the church needed. Some days this meant he was insulating pipes in my house. Other days he was babysitting my kids, or other kids from the congregation, even though he didn't know a thing about watching kids. He said "yes" to anything.

He had a servant's heart.

At about the six-month mark, Deb Fitch broached the topic at a board meeting.

"Marvin's one-year commitment is almost up – what are we going to do without him?"

"Guys," I said, "this church isn't even paying me yet. I've had to raise all the money for my salary. We are barely making our bills."

She looked at the rest of the board members.

"Okay, how many of you folks around this table would give a little extra to keep Marvin?"

"Sure," said one person.

"Yeah, we'll give extra," said another.

"Let's do the little tablet thing," she said. "Gerry, do you have your tablet? Pass it around. Everyone put down your name and what you will give monthly to keep Marvin."

Marvin had collected a little salary by the end of that meeting.

They were desperate to keep him because he provided what money couldn't buy: he encouraged each one of them, he spoke into their lives prophetically, he probably mowed all of their grass at some point by the end of that first summer (even the ones he didn't live with), he helped them with their businesses. He gave everything that could be given.

At the end of that the church said, "One way or another, we've got to keep Marvin."

This is a perfect example of a worker deserving their pay.

I've told Marvin's story to everyone who has ever wanted to join my staff. I just finished going through this with my son Luke.

"Luke, you want to be on staff? Great. Here's the thing. I'm never going to persuade people to hire you. If you don't persuade them by what you provide, it won't happen."

At the end of a finance team meeting recently, I asked if anyone else had an agenda item they'd like to discuss.

"I've got something," the woman who was in charge of our youth said. "It's a little awkward, but we need to do something about Luke."

I froze.

"What's wrong with him?" I asked.

"There's nothing wrong," she said. "The thing is, he's talking about going to get a job, but I need him to run our youth group. I need him!"

"Really? Tell me about that."

"I think if he's working, I'm going to lose momentum, and I don't think I could run the youth group without him."

"What's it worth to you?"

"One way or another, we've got to pay him what he's making at work. We can replace that, right?"

Everyone around the room nodded.

"If he's producing like that," someone said, "then we need him."

I say this to all the young folks at our church: anyone here can earn a spot. Anyone can earn a right to get paid.

A worker deserves his wages.

Serve your way into the body of Christ, until the body says "we need to give back."

Chapter Eleven: Be A Healer

"Heal the sick..."

Jesus said, "Wherever you go, heal the sick, and tell them the kingdom of heaven is near you." This tells me that there are two specific jobs for every believer, and one of them is to be a healer. I don't think, based on Jesus life, that he is just talking about physical healing – he's also saying that we're not troublemakers, we're not rabble rousers, we're healers.

Healing needs to be our approach to life.

We should always be healing. How can we do any less, given our orders to heal, and our God-given ability to do just that? Scripture calls us repairers of the breach, which I think is talking about the space between God and people but also those spaces between individuals. We are always interested in how we can get a marriage working or get that child talking to their parent again. How can we help create an environment where people can connect with each other in a way that heals their view of life?

The healer part needs to be applied to a person's entire life.

God's people need to be people who heal.

I got a really cool note from a high school guidance counselor a few years ago. In an email he said:

Mr. & Mrs. Stoltzfoos,

I am long overdue in thanking you for the impact that I see your church having on this community. As a counselor here at New Oxford High School I can tell you that time and again, you have helped to connect so many of our students with a solid foundation. Time and again your church's name comes up in conversations with students and parents and the more I learn about your church, the more I appreciate the different ways in which you connect with teenagers.

I wept over this letter – it was so powerful to me.

That's our goal – to be a church that is healing in its approach to life. Let's be honest: confrontation is part of the gospel, but it's not the goal of the gospel. Confrontation and offense will often occur when you are spreading the gospel message, but it can never be the goal.

Let me share another letter that illustrates some healing that took place in a young girl's life. This girl came to the Harvest Cry event we hold every year. This is what she wrote to us on Facebook:

I wanted to thank you for inviting me to come out tonight. At first I felt a little out of place, not knowing anyone, but after a while I kinda realized it's not about who knows who here, or how stupid I may look standing there when everyone's clapping their hands. Everyone was there for one reason. And that was to love and believe in and cry out to Jesus Christ.

I can't thank you enough for saying something about comin' out, because I had one of the best nights of my life. Do you by chance know how I could contact the young girl that, I'm not sure if you saw, but the girl that pulled me aside and talked to me and prayed for me...over by the steps to the stage...she's also the girl that said she gave herself to Jesus Christ a year ago and things have been much easier for her. I can't remember her name.

BUT JEEZE-O I'm so happy I went. I'd love to go back. Everyone makes you feel so loved there. Your freaking pastor came over and said, "Hi, what's your name?" and I'm all shy, like, Megan, and he's like, "Oh, hi Megan, who are you with?" and I pointed at Alex and he shook my hand and said "Thanks for coming!" and then he said I love you and I was like fdakjlfjafdfda! holy shit!

fdklajf;la! Freedom Valley Center is the number one church in the world. Ha I feel a lot better about myself.

I read that letter to my staff last year, weeping.

"I'm sorry," I said, "but I've got to read it to you as it is, language and all."

That is the kind of healing the church has to offer.

But it's not just about emotional healing. I get the feeling these days that a lot of Christians are uncomfortable with the idea of physical healing. Jesus makes it clear, though, that he sent his followers out to be healers. This includes physical healing.

Let me tell you about my feet.

I have always had flat feet. And they're size 14. They're gargantuan, and Merrill Smucker, my good friend, loves to make fun of them. One time when we were riding our motorcycles together, I noticed he was laughing his head off.

"What is your problem?" I asked him when we stopped at a red light.

"When you put your feet up there on those highway pegs, you're creating wind turbulence for us back here. You've got to put those things down!"

He and I laughed for three days about that.

All that to say, I've got large feet.

I went to a podiatrist because I had been riding at our therapeutic riding arena on a horse. I rode a lot when I was a kid, so I'm comfortable on a horse, but in this case Brandy had me trick riding. The trick she wanted me to do was to jump off the horse at a full gallop and then back on and off and on as it goes around the arena. One time I came down and the horse stepped on the instep of my foot. I was in a lot of pain. So I went to the podiatrist.

"I've been meaning to come here for years," I said. "I've had problems with foot pain for as long as I can remember – pretty much every step I've taken since I was 12 or 13 has hurt. For the last few years I've been in so much pain from standing up all day Sunday, I could barely walk until Wednesday. I need to know what's going on."

So he x-rayed my foot.

"Well, you have no arches," he said at my next appointment. "We're going to take a few more x-rays. But it looks like you're going to need an operation to repair your feet. It's $4,000 for each foot, and the recovery time is six weeks. Most insurance companies don't cover it – they consider it elective, even though it's only recommended when pain levels are so high that it's actually required."

That was hard to hear. How could I take 12 weeks off for my feet?

Where was I going to come up with $8,000?

"Why don't we start with prosthetic arches?" he suggested. "It could delay the surgery, lessen your pain a bit. And that's the whole goal. Those arches don't always work, but it's probably worth a try."

So that's what we decided to do. I started putting on my jacket and prepared to leave his office.

"By the way," the doctor said. "I heard one of the nurses refer to you as pastor."

I nodded.

"Well, has your church prayed over you?"

I hesitated a little bit.

"Maybe your church doesn't believe in healing," he continued.

I started blushing.

"Pastor, if you want," he continued, "my church believes in healing. You can come on over and we'll pray for you!"

I had seen so many miracles in my life – I was embarrassed to admit that I had never asked anyone to pray over me about my hurting feet! How could that be possible? I left there shamefaced and arrived at the church a few minutes later. Marvin, Cindy, Connie and a few others were standing in the lobby when I arrived.

"Would you folks pray for me? I've just been told that I need this huge surgery, $4,000 for each foot, a major operation that would put me in a wheel chair for up to 12 weeks. Plus the doctor asked why I haven't had anyone pray over me."

They prayed for me. I walked out that day, still limping just because I always had been. A few days later I thought to myself, *"I've been sleeping really well at night. I wonder why?*

Then it hit me.

My feet didn't hurt, at all. And they haven't at any point since. I've not had one day of arch pain since then.

The church has so much healing to offer a hurting world.

A few years ago, I was leading a dreaming session with a group of new leaders. I encouraged them to dream about how we could be healers in our world.

We used a set of questions to think through the possibilities: What could be possible if there was no lack of money, or time?

Brandy Crago approached me after that session.

"I'd like to tell you about my answer to that question," she said. "If there was no lack of money or time, I would start a ministry for handicapped children, using horses to help them. I heard about this somewhere, and I want to help."

Brandy had been a world champion trick rider, in the past, jumping off and back on galloping horses, doing headstands on the back of a horse, as well as other amazing tricks.

"So listen, I get that you know about horses," I told her. "But what are you talking about with this ministry?"

I have to be honest: I thought the idea was a little crazy.

"Riding horses provides stimulation, physical therapy, and an opportunity for caring volunteers to minister to the kids," she explained.

Brandy has been ministering to those kids ever since. Today we have around 150 volunteers helping out about 80 students each summer. Soon we hope to build an indoor riding arena where kids can come year round.

Healers get God's attention because that's who he's called us to be.

Melisa Leventry had a healing heart like that. We first met her as a student in Gettysburg Master's Commission. She seemed frustrated with life, and angry about so many things that she had to face. But in Master's Commission, we saw Melissa transformed by the power of God. She let her Heavenly dad heal her heart and restore her soul. We watched with excitement as the anger faded, replaced by a desire to help others heal.

Her first year of Master's Commission ended, but Melissa chose to stay on as a second year student, in charge of mentoring a couple of new students who were hurting as much as she had been in her first year. Her third year, she became a leader. She started a summer ministry to high school kids to help them navigate through their own pain.

Then the day came when she told me that she was called back to her hometown, Pittsburgh, to be a healer there. I was very sad about losing her incredible heart for students, but was willing to bless her in going, and even excited about what God would do with her healing gift in a new city.

A few months later I got a call from her.

"We started a ministry in a downtown tattoo parlor on East Carson street," she told me, "and kids are coming to Jesus! You gotta come and see this."

You can't stretch a former Beachy-Amish kid much further than doing ministry in a tattoo parlor. There was nothing about the tattoo world that interested me. Except kids coming to Jesus and getting healed.

So I went. The Bible study was held on a Monday night. I met a young man that I'll call Mitchell. Mitchell was one of the first attendees to the Bible-study-in-a-tattoo-parlor, and one of the first to move closer to Jesus with a public confession of faith.

Then I met 50 of Mitchell's friends: 50! I kept moving back further into those tattoo chairs, past the piercing room, and still they kept coming. They were sitting on the floor, on the chairs, everywhere they could. Then Mitchell stood up to speak, telling about what God was doing in his heart.

I couldn't see Mitchell from the back corner where I ended up, but I could hear him talk about his anger being healed, and his frustrations melting away because of his faith in Christ. I heard him call out to kids to make a choice to follow their Creator. Way in the back of that tattoo parlor, tears were running down my cheeks.

A few weeks later Melissa called me again. "We have a problem," she told me.

"Really?" I asked. "What's the problem?"

"The lady who owns the tattoo parlor is selling the place. I don't know what we are going to do to keep this Bible study going. We have been all over the East Carson Street area and couldn't find another place to meet. I don't know what to do," Melissa explained quietly.

"So how can I help, Melissa?"

"Gerry, I wonder if you would help me buy the tattoo parlor?" Melissa said.

Silence.

I never wanted to own a tattoo parlor. This is not in my top ten goals for life. Or the top fifty. Okay, I admit: it never entered my mind. Even after considering this thought for the first time, I still didn't want it! But I promised Jesus that I would do anything I could to get a few more people to Heaven. Anything. So we helped her. For a short time, we secured a note to make that purchase possible.

I went out to one of the opening Monday night meetings. The Bible study was strong, and young adults were clearly being moved and healed in Christ. That evening as we went out to eat after the Bible study, we saw a police officer and someone told him about the church's involvement at the tattoo parlor. His eyebrows raised.

"I'm glad somebody did something there", he said with an odd expression on his face. "A lot of bad stuff came from that place."

Later, we found out that the basement to that place had been a sadomasochism dungeon. We also heard a lot of other things that may or may not have been true. But what we knew for sure was that one unlikely place on East Carson Street in Pittsburgh was now a place where young adults were finding Jesus, finding healing. All because of Melissa's healing heart and the healing hearts of her friends.

Healers are not just people who can describe a problem. Anyone can do that. Healers are people who imagine a solution. They choose the more courageous path – thinking about what it might take for the situation to come out better than it is presently.

Prayer, for a healer, is not a recitation of spiritual niceties. Prayer is the opportunity to connect with God in imagining what miracle might make the situation better, and what circumstances would be required for that miracle to be received. Healers build environments conducive to the healing process, and work to understand the illnesses presented to them so that they can know something of what to ask for in seeing it remedied.

Healers are not seeking to be fed as much as whom to feed. They see their own success rooted in helping others find success. Instead of wanting to remove their critics and adversaries, they ask God for the miracle of winning that person over, and seeing their hurting hearts healed.

Healers can't ask themselves, "Is this fun for me?" Instead they ask, "Is anyone being helped?"

Unfortunately, healers are a rare commodity in any church. A church full of them would rock the earth.

Chapter Twelve: A Very Simple Message

"The Kingdom of God is near you now!"

Let me take you back a few years, to 1992, when Julie and I first attempted to plant a church.

Julie and I originally wanted to plant a church in Philadelphia; in fact, we had a vision to plant ten churches in the Philly area. I spent more than six months scouring the city. You have to remember, there was no Google back then, so all the demographic research had to be done at the library or local chambers of commerce. It was hard work, and laborious.

We finally settled on a plan to start in the suburbs, because that's where the money is, and then use that as a launching point into the inner city. But something wasn't quite coming together. God had given me three parameters when it came to planting a church: first it had to be able to support my family; second of all, it needed to be in a growing community, not a diminishing community (there were quite a few diminishing communities outside of Philadelphia in the early nineties); finally, there had to be a group already praying for a new church. These were big to me – Julie and I felt that God had given us these directions, and we were committed to sticking to them.

After finishing our assignment at Victory Chapel, we spent all of our severance pay searching Philadelphia. Community after community, and we still couldn't find the right one. So, finally, we decided we were going to plant in the Willow Grove area – this seemed the closest we could get to it being right. But we were still lacking that third parameter. We couldn't find a group of people praying for a new church.

Around that time I got a letter from Jeff Kettering. He worked for the Assembly of God sectional team in central Pennsylvania. He and I had been youth pastors together in years gone by, and we were in a cordial, friendly relationship. In the meantime he had gone on to pastor a church.

He wrote me a letter that went something like this:

Gerry,

Our section wants to plant a church and we heard you are thinking about planting a church. Would you consider our area? There are six towns we'd like you to think about: New Oxford, McSherrystown, Cashtown, Aspers, Biglerville and Littlestown.

I didn't get much further in reading the letter. *Where in the world is this guy located, and where are these towns he is talking about? I've never heard of them! If I haven't heard of the towns, has anyone?* I wanted to plant a church in a significant place, not someplace like New Oxford. If I told people that I was planting a church in Philadelphia, they immediately knew what I was talking about – you say "New Oxford"? No one has a clue.

I didn't give the letter ten seconds of thought. But I do still remember balling it up and throwing it in the trash. *No way*, I thought, *I'm not going to some insignificant place.*

One week later Jeff called me.

"Why didn't you answer my letter?"

"Jeff, God told me to plant a church in Philadelphia. Do you want to help? You could finance my church. The next thing I need to do is raise money."

115

"Yeah," he said, "we've got money saved up and we want to help. But not in Philly. We want to plant out here."

"That's great," I said. "But I'm pretty sure my call is Philadelphia."

A moment of silence. We were just going around in circles.

"Could you just answer the letter?" he asked.

"Jeff, my answer is no."

He got quiet for a moment, then continued.

"Then I don't know what to do with this," he said.

"Do with what?"

"Well, we had a meeting and God spoke to us about you, specifically."

"What?"

Everyone was trying to tell me what God was saying in those days, and I wasn't sure if I was buying any of it.

"I'm praying like crazy," I said, "so why wouldn't God say that to me? I read your letter, and I didn't feel anything."

"Maybe God spoke to us about you because you have some wisdom that you need to give us about planting churches."

That spoke to the youthful, prideful part of me – they want wisdom from me? I didn't think anyone wanted my wisdom at that point in my life. If they thought I had wisdom, maybe I should pay attention.

"Listen," he said. "This is so big to us, and we feel so sure you're our guy, that we want you to meet with us in Gettysburg."

Huh, I've heard of Gettysburg.

"We could meet at the Heritage Assembly Church in Gettysburg," he continued.

"I guess it wouldn't hurt to meet," I said.

Julie and I drove out to Gettysburg. I was in the passenger seat pouring over maps and information borrowed from local chambers of commerce. Demographic studies littered the front dash. I had actually borrowed the Chester County Chamber of Commerce's hard copy of the Adams County demographics – when I went to the office, they didn't have a copy machine (many of you might not remember these days), so they loaned me their hard copy (there were some threats involved as to what would happen if they didn't get it back).

So we entered the little town of New Oxford. I poured over the demographics and maps while Julie drove. Suddenly Julie hit the brakes pretty hard, startling me.

I looked up from my papers – no traffic, no stoplight. But she had stopped in the middle of the road.

"Babe, what are you doing?" I asked.

"Do you see that house?"

"Yeah."

"That's our house."

"What?"

"I just got a picture in my mind of us living in that house," she said with an amazed look on her face. "I even saw our kids, but they were older, playing in the backyard."

Up to that moment, she and I were totally committed to moving to Philadelphia. Up to that moment.

"That's crazy!" I said. "That house would be too expensive to move to Philadelphia. And why would we? It's not even a nice house! Is that your dream house?"

"No," she said. "I don't even really like that house."

I just shook my head.

"That's the craziest thing ever," I continued, only half joking. "But maybe we can move that house to Philadelphia."

"No, no, no," she said. "The picture I got was of the kids growing up in that back yard."

"Does it even have a backyard?" I asked.

"I don't know, but I saw it."

Each time I tell this story, I get chills, and I remember how I felt that day, as if my brain was turning inside my skull. Everything we felt so determined about began to shift. Everything we thought we knew about our calling suddenly felt less certain, more flexible.

"I am not planting a church in New Oxford," I said.

"I know," she said, "but that's what I saw."

So we traveled 13 miles further west to the meeting at Heritage Assembly of God on the other side of Gettysburg. I walked in and looked around. Up until that point, my friend Jeff had only told me that a group of pastors were planning on planting a church. Just a group in this community that believed church planting was a powerful way to reach people. They sounded like my kind of folks.

I walked into a somewhat traditional-looking church, an Assembly of God church, and when I entered the room where we were meeting, there were eight guys around a table.

"Are you all from the Assemblies of God denomination?" I asked as I sat down at my chair.

The guy who was running the meeting looked at me and nodded.

"Yes, we're all pastors of Assembly churches. Why?"

I kind of hesitated.

"I don't know, guys. I don't mean to be unkind, but let me just get my cards on the table right from the start: I don't like the Assemblies of God."

They kind of looked at each other, and one of them spoke up.

"Why?"

"Well, here's the thing. I think the Assemblies of God is arrogant. I think you're not reaching people but you think you are. I think you create systems to keep people out of church – a lot like the Beachy-Amish background I came from. I don't want to be in a system that keeps people out of church!"

The sectional presbyter of the Assemblies looked at the table for a moment, then he reached up and took off his glasses and let them hang on the chain around his neck.

"Young man," he said. "Let me just tell you this: I don't like the Assemblies of God either. I'm here because I like Jesus. If you like Jesus, then let's talk. If you want to plant a church someday that truly lifts up the name of Jesus and makes him great, then let's talk. If you don't, God bless you."

That was the one thing in the world he could have said that would have kept me at that table.

"Well, yeah, I like Jesus," I said.

"I know," he said. "We checked you out. We know that you like Jesus, and we know that where you go, people around you like Jesus. Now if you want to talk, let's talk."

"Okay, I'm listening."

"We have a passion in our hearts to plant a church in this community. This county has started growing a lot."

A little bell went off in my head – one of my parameters was met (plant a church in a growing community).

"We want to help you provide for your family so that you can plant a church," he continued.

Ding! A second parameter was also met: being able to provide for my family.

"And we have a group of people meeting monthly to pray for a new pastor and a new church."

I can only imagine the look on my face when he unknowingly stated all three of my parameters in the first few minutes of our time together. I nearly fell back off my chair. *This is crazy,* I thought to myself. *I don't want to be Assembly, I don't want to be in New Oxford, I've never heard of this community before. I couldn't even offend them! I tried, and they responded to me with love and grace!*

We talked for a long time. At the end of the meeting the sectional presbyter spoke up again.

"Here's $100 for you, young man. I know you've come a long way. This is enough money for you and your family to have lunch and dinner here, and to pay for your gas."

Julie and the kids were waiting outside.

"You can take a few more trips out here if you want," he continued. "But we want you to pray about being the pastor of this new church. God already spoke to us about you, so if you take it, you're hired. That's it. We'll do it. But we will never call you again, or write you again, or bother you again. If you don't want to do it, this is it. The money is yours – enjoy it. Call us by the end of the week if you are interested."

Julie and I spent the rest of that day driving around the county, praying. We took the kids to McDonald's. We stopped and talked to a couple of pastors. We stopped at a builder outside of town to talk about the price of buildings – I figured planting a church meant putting up a building.

"I just got saved while building a church a few years ago," he said. "This is exciting – I'd like to work with you."

He ended up constructing our new church building, seven years later.

By the end of the day, I knew, and I told Julie.

"Too many things have happened here. Too much, too powerfully – it's changed my heart and my mind. This is going to be where we plant our church."

I waited another day before I called the men back. I tend to be a little action-oriented, so I figured it wouldn't hurt to wait a bit before responding. I wanted to slow down a little and think it through.

But the next day Julie and I talked again, and she gave me the final push.

"That's where we should plant a church. That's our place. That house is ours. Let's do it."

We did end up buying that house, by the way. The next time that we drove through Adam's County, there was a For Sale By Owner sign out front. I called the number. The owner, John Kulp, was very nice and interested in helping us. That is, he was interested until I told him the rest of the story.

I told him that I had no job and was moving into the community to start a church. He responded that he had never heard of churches being started.

"They all have to start sometime I guess," he said. "I just haven't heard of it in my lifetime."

He told me to go to a bank and take out a loan, and he'd be happy to sell us his house. My heart sank, knowing that no bank would like our situation. But I went anyway.

When the bank turned me down, I called John back.

"I didn't get the loan, John, but I still want to buy your house. God spoke to me about it, and I think I am supposed to have it."

"God spoke to you?" John asked. "He does that? Isn't that a little weird?"

I wasn't sure what to say.

"I never heard of that, either," he continued. "Young man, get your money together and give me a call. But if the bank isn't willing to take a risk on you, neither am I. Sorry."

He hung up.

I went out to the little shed-office that Galen Smoker had given me, in which he had started his own business years earlier.

"Now what?" I asked God. Suddenly the answer came. I picked up the phone again, and dialed John Culp's number.

"I want to buy your house," I told him again, persistent. "Help me find a way to do it. I am a hard worker and will do whatever it takes to pay for that house. I will work 3 jobs if I have to, or anything else. I have never been even late for one single payment ever, and never will be. Take a risk on me and you will not regret it."

I don't know why, but John Culp did help. He found a way to finance the sale himself, even borrowing money to do it. Julie's parents helped, too, with the down payment.

We still live there, 18 years later, in our miracle house. It's still not a great house, but it's ours. And it is a huge reminder of God's ability to create a way for me to succeed in what He called me to do.

So we decided to plant our church in Adams County.

Another church in Adams County?

A quick look in the yellow pages and I discovered 80 churches in Adams County, a county whose population was about 80,000. Why plant a church where there are lots and lots of churches? So we got the whole church together – basically Julie and I at that point! – and started fasting and praying.

"God, we're sure you've called us to Adams County – why? There appear to be some great churches here. They're Bible-believing, life-changing, life-giving churches. What do we have to add?"

About that time a Newsweek magazine came to my house that had a cover story about faith in America. As I recall, there was an article that said something along the lines that America is changing, and the primary force of change is that Americans are walking out of churches. This was in the fall of 1991.

Americans are walking out of churches left and right, the article said, and it appears that it could be a tsunami of people leaving the church. The article said that at that point four out of ten Americans used to go to church but didn't anymore. Taking Jesus' teaching at the parable where he left the 99 to find the lost one and transforming it into numbers for today, it was as if that shepherd had lost 40 sheep! You couldn't even call him a good shepherd anymore.

There doesn't seem, the writer continued, to be a group or a denomination going after those lost sheep.

When I read this it felt like a sledge hammer between the eyes.

I ran into the house and found Julie.

"You're not going to believe this article," I said.

"Why is this article so important?" she asked as she took the magazine from me and started looking at it.

"Because it's the church God wants us to plant. It's for hurt people, people hurt by their church like we were hurt by our own church. That's what God wants to do – reach people like us."

I had gone through a time of questioning the whole idea of church. *Maybe all church is wrong,* I thought to myself. *Maybe the whole concept is off. Maybe in America we are so far from what Jesus wanted that no churches are Christ like.* I went through a whole soul-searching thing, crying my way through service after service.

But then, through that article, the Holy Spirit showed me that this was what church was for.

Rick Warren did some research for "The Purpose Driven Church" and gave us the top 10 reasons people don't go to church anymore. They were things like: the church doesn't help me; the church feels like something from hundreds of years ago, not today; the music is old; I don't understand the Bible.

I don't remember the exact reasons as much as I remember thinking, *These are fixable issues! We can make this better! Some of those lost sheep will try again if they are invited back to a changed environment!*

Now we're getting somewhere, I thought. *This is the church that God wants us to start, a church that will deal with these issues head on. A church that contributes to every other church in Adams County. A church that competes with none of them because it is helping each of them win back those that they lost!* I was getting excited.

What would it look like if we started a church for these people?

We started asking the question often: What would it look like to start a church for people who have given up on church? And God provided the stories to help with the preparation. There was a youth leader whose youth group had grown large and had threatened the Pastor's popularity. The youth leader was asked to leave the church. There was the pastor who, we were told, had an affair. Three families were devastated, and that church split with so much pain.

There were so many who felt like church bored them, or did not apply to what they were facing. People who had a bad experience of one kind or another and never wanted to go back to church, ever. There were those who never felt like they were good enough to be used as leaders, and those who felt too many scars from the last time they tried to lead. And there were still others who felt abused by a leadership decision.

Some had given up on church without ever trying.

It became our battle cry and still is today. Except for one thing: the numbers have changed. Years after the Newsweek article, Barna's research firm put the number of those not attending church much, much higher. Recently, I heard some pastors guessing that not more than 10% of the American population attends church.

I think they may be right.

So we started seeking solutions. Our message was to make The Kingdom available to those who have given up on church. To reach people who once thought about church, or whose parents attended but gradually gave up. We also wanted to reach those who never considered church because they never got to be around people who encouraged them to turn to their Creator in time of trouble.

Yet America continues leaving church.

.

As Freedom Valley got off to a fledging start, these numbers kicked my spirit into high gear. Church planting reaches people who are not going to church. In fact, new churches reach people far better than those who have been in existence for a long time. Some theorists and researchers noticed that there is a direct correlation between the age of a church and how effective it is at reaching unchurched people.

This became our new problem: we were growing older. As we did, I was desperate to continue to be the kind of church that reached more lost people, not less.

I hungered to plant more life-giving churches.

Our first attempts at church planting were more about helping someone else plant. We count them as ours in the sense that we invested something very precious to us: sometimes money, sometimes people, sometimes prayer and support. But we had no control over them or influence into how they operated or what kind of church they were. We were simply excited about helping somebody start another place that would help us reach our world.

Upon This Rock, for example, is not a church that we had a huge role in planting, but I feel it was very important to us in that we were only a church of about 80 people at the time. I heard that there was a guy in my neighborhood who wanted to plant a church. To be honest, I initially felt very threatened. We were young and fledgling and had just gotten started, and our church's income was only just about enough to pay my salary.

But I also felt that if I didn't get used to pushing myself outside of my comfort zone a lot in the early days, I would never be able to plant churches. Pastor Leith Anderson's words kept ringing in my ears: he always said that any church over 40 should be planting other churches. Most people think that's ridiculous;

most think your weekly attendance should be over 500 before you plant. But I have this theory: most churches never get to that point UNLESS they plant a church!

If more pastors could see planting as a church growth tool, I think it would help them a lot. How can sending out people and resources and finances be a church GROWTH tool? This is how: I think it shows the Holy Spirit that you are serious about growing the kingdom, not just about growing your own church. And I think God will bless that.

After all, Jesus is the builder of the church.

So, Upon This Rock is the first church plant we were involved in. The guy's name was Jeff Wolf. He lives just a few houses away from me. I wanted to be involved, so I looked him up.

"Jeff," I said, "I think I can help."

He may have thought I was nuts. He probably wondered how a church with 80 people would make any meaningful contribution to his new church.

"Okay," he said. "I could use a worship team, and we could definitely use some money."

I can't remember exactly how much money we gave them but I do remember this – it was everything we had in our little account at that point. I think it was around $750. And I gave him a worship team and a sound system.

He was ecstatic.

And that's all that we ever gave them. He never asked for much in the way of meeting up or getting together to talk, and that was cool. I would imagine he never saw himself as a church plant of ours, or under us in any way – I'm sure we were too insignificant. And I was fine with that.

I kept hearing something Omar used to say as he mentored me: "It's amazing what we could get done if we stopped caring about who gets the credit". I was trying very hard to be that guy, the one who didn't care about who got the credit.

To this day it's not a massive church in size. But looking back, I've realized that our role in Upon This Rock had much less to do with building that church than it did with getting our hearts right. We needed to stretch ourselves, prove to ourselves, and to the Holy Spirit, that we were kingdom players. My efforts as a pastor can never primarily be about building Freedom Valley. It just can't. So we did our best to help, release those resources, and move on.

I'm not saying it didn't cost us – we sent some worship people which put our full band down to two pieces again, and I had to rebuild the team. I lost two children's workers, which are always the hardest to replace. Every church plant we send out children's workers, and my remaining children's team weeps. It is so hard for them. The volunteers in the children's team are probably the people who pay the dearest when we plant a church, because they have to rebuild their team every time, and it's extra Sundays in the rotation until they do. They are my heroes.

We're even experimenting, in some of our newer plants, with paying the prime children's worker before anyone else, even the head pastor. That's how important these leaders are to a new church. We can't afford for that to be flimsy.

Our second plant was a project with our section – Christian Life Church in Shippensburg. I was in some discussions when they said they wanted to plant another church in our area.

"That's exciting!" I said. "I want to help."

"Well," they said, "you're too new to help formally, but informally you can give us a hand."

This still makes me smile.

So informally I met with the pastor every week for a while, then every other week, then every month. His request was to be with someone who had planted a church, because the whole concept was still so new to all of us back then. Really rare. It was hard to find someone who had done it with any dimension of success.

He needed encouragement, so I tried to give what he asked for.. And we gave financially, maybe $200 a month or something along those lines. The same churches that helped us when we got started also helped him. These are the same people that put together a war chest of $30,000 and prayed regularly for a new church – this was so gutsy and forward thinking in the early nineties. Jeff Kettering is a real Kingdom leader who is still catalyzing great kingdom stuff in these ways.

So Christian Life Church started in Shippensburg with Pastor Steve Wolf. He did really well – they are probably a church of 200 or 300 now. Recently Steve asked for our help again, this time to plant in Tampa. He is an amazing leader.

But not everything has been smooth and easy.

After helping out with Upon This Rock, there were two churches that we tried to help that just didn't make it. We heard about these baby churches that were starting up, so we contacted them and asked, "How can we help?"

One of them was started by a local guy. He was doing great and built the church up to 70 or 80 people. I gave him a call one Sunday afternoon.

"Hey, how's the church going? I had you on my heart today and wanted to check in to see how you're doing."

"Oh, that might be because we closed it."

"What?" I was shocked. "Why would you close a church?"

"Yeah, it's been a little rough lately and we decided we didn't want to put up with it anymore so we just closed it. Today."

I couldn't revive that church. We tried, but by then most of the people were gone, and we couldn't bring it back to life. I was (am) heartbroken. It still hurts, in the way it hurts years later when we lose a loved one.

When I look back at churches that didn't make it, I try to figure out what went wrong, if only to help in our future church plants. The first thing I notice is usually a lack of planning: we really expected the Holy Spirit to kick in and carry it, and the Holy Spirit said, *No, I expect you to kick in and carry this.*

They weren't financed particularly well, either. Dr. Ed Stetzer says the Assemblies church plants tend to be one of the lowest-financed church plants in the world, but also the best. More churches succeed in the Assemblies than in any other denomination, he says, so I was thinking within this model that

127

maybe it's healthier for the churches to pull themselves up by their boot straps. But it wasn't smart in these situations.

The churches that didn't succeed also weren't networked with other churches and pastors and local leaders. Accountability was too loose, and this leads to feelings of isolation and vulnerability. I remember how that felt, first arriving in New Oxford and struggling to fit in: wishing the phone would ring, even if it was a telemarketer. It's not a good feeling, and it doesn't facilitate a strong beginning for a new church.

Also important is to look at the motivation of the person planting the church – are they planting because they want to expand the Kingdom of God, or are they planting because they have a grudge against their previous church and want to do things their own way? Young leaders are often more angry with the church than they are filled with a vision to do something good. All of us have some of that – there is a healthy amount of resistance which breeds fresh vision. I think you have to be a little skeptical, and willing to explore and evaluate success. But if the planter's primary motivation is anger or revenge, it's not going to work.

I think you have to be healthy enough to love at least the idea of church.

The next church was Liberty Worship Center – this is probably the first one that was mostly considered ours, at least in the beginning. But I also get the most grief about this church because of some key mistakes we made early on.

Around 1995 I had a group of people approach me who were attending our church for about six months, and they asked if they could meet with me and talk about planting a new church in Fairfield, about ten miles west of Gettysburg. This is one of the fastest growing communities in Adams County, Pennsylvania and a very nice community. We thought it would be a really great place to plant a church.

There was a core group of people, three or four families, who wanted a church planted there. So I met with them and discovered that for a while they had been part of a Baptist Church in that area. Then I met with the Baptist pastor.

"Yeah," he said, "these people are not happy with me. They want a more spirit-filled church. I've encouraged them to start a church."

To this day I get a lot of grief about that church in Fairfield. It's almost inevitable that if I talk about church planting with any pastor in this county, they will bring up the fact that I'm "not nice" when I plant churches.

"We heard about how you started that church in Fairfield with so many people from the Baptist church," they say. "We hear that's how you start churches, is by taking people from other churches." I guess a rumor somehow got started that I persuaded those original families to leave the Baptist church and come start a new church with us. That is so far from the truth.

There are some key details that I didn't know at the time – I didn't know that one of these people who started the church in Fairfield was a youth pastor from the Baptist church, and another was a worship leader. I didn't know these things. And they certainly didn't convey that to me, or maybe I didn't listen well enough. I would never knowingly take anyone from any church.

Anyway, this church met in a home for a while and grew to 25 or 30 people. Then it moved into a public venue, and for about six months we organized and put it together as a preaching station, or an outflow of our church. We arranged the service times so that I could drive out there, about a 20-minute drive, and preach between our two services, and still get back in time to preach our second service.

Then our associate pastor Marvin did that for about a year. After almost two years, we found a full-time pastor, and he's still there today. They are now finishing their first building, which is really cool.

They were also the first church to come back and say, "We don't want to be connected to Freedom Valley anymore." So they're not connected to us in any way. The pastor felt it would be better to be separate.

This can be a little difficult, when a church you planted comes back and says that. It feels a little like rejection, but if you insist that your heart stays kingdom-focused and doesn't try for ownership of your church plants, then it's okay. There are simply too many people to reach to waste time choosing to feel hurt.

I use it as an example for anyone in our church interested in planting a new one. I assure my young guys that I'm not a control guy. I even tell our own sites that any time, any day, they want to be autonomous, they are welcome to do their own thing. It's theirs. And there will never be retribution of any kind for that.

Liberty Worship Center is my prime example and proof of something very important to a young leader- we want to help, not control.

I do some things differently now, after our experience with Liberty Worship Center. For example, I've become much more deliberate about meeting with pastors in the vicinity of the planned church-plant.

But timing is such a touchy thing when you're meeting with leaders of churches, and here's why: if I meet with them too early and tell them we're going to plant a church but then don't do it, they call me a liar. I had one pastor who, whenever he saw me, he'd say, "Gerry, you're always saying stuff you don't do." Well, this is because I was trying too hard to keep him in the loop, and I guess I was telling him things too early.

But if you tell people too late, then they don't feel like they're part of the process – they say I'm not really meeting with them to get input, I'm just meeting with them to inform them.

I've realized that no matter what, a church planter will get criticized every step of the way. So the best I can do, when I meet with pastors of churches in areas where we're going to plant, is assure them we are not going to take any of their people. I have a whole spiel I run through with our own people, in our own congregation, telling them to make sure they don't invite people from other churches to our church plants – if you find out that a visitor goes to another church, don't follow up with them.

We don't even greet them! We're practically mean to visitors if we find out they're from another church, just because we try so hard to be sensitive to local pastors!

I had a young lady approach me this year.

"May I come to your church?" she asked.

"Of course you 'may'. What do you mean?"

"Well, I used to go to this other church . . ."

"Oh," I interrupted her. "That does present a problem."

"I feel like you guys don't even want me here," she said.

"Well, we really don't want to take people from other churches."

"But I'm not going to that church anymore!"

"Listen, if you're feeling called here, if you're feeling like this is important to you, then you're welcome with open arms, but we tend to push people away if they're coming from other churches because we're trying hard to show other churches that we're not trying to grow that way."

Consequently, Freedom Valley has baptized about 1500 people so far, about 80% of current church attendance. Most of our people are new to church, and that's the way we prefer it.

But we can't always know exactly where people are coming from.

Some folks say, "No, I have no church background," but they've been attending somewhere for a year. Even though they haven't accepted that church as their home church, the folks at that church have seen them for a year and assumed they're family and counted on them. Then they disappear, and show up at my church, and suddenly I'm considered a people-stealer.

So we spend a lot of time with pastors while we are planting, trying to help them feel okay, help them understand that we want to expand the Kingdom of Heaven, not rob them of their members.

We just opened The Intersection – it's one of our newest sites. I wrote a personal email to every pastor in the community that I could think of and wrote them a personal note something along the lines of:

"Dear Pastor, I want you to know that it looks like we are going to move towards opening a new site in the area. I let you guys know a year or so ago that we hoped to do this, and it looks like it's coming together. The new site is called The Intersection and they're going to meet in our building for a while until they get their own building. They are hoping to be in Gettysburg, although they've also explored New Oxford and Hanover. And they're still exploring those areas. We don't know where they'll be, but as soon as we know, we'll try to keep you informed."

The response was mostly good, although a few pastors did remind me of the Liberty Worship Center church in Fairfield, that we planted maybe 12 years ago.

"We know earlier you planted churches and invited other church leaders to attend," they wrote, "and that was really, really hurtful to those churches."

I'm hoping with The Intersection, since it's starting in our building with our people, that I can prove to them it's not about taking their people. Which brings me to one of the main reasons we love to plant churches:

I'm always looking for ways to empty our seats. We want to get church people out of our pews, not fill them with church people! Over 70% is too full, and I can't do endless services well – we've tried as many as five in a weekend. I burn out, my long-suffering, hard-working staff burns out, and I'm not relational enough. The people on my team roll their eyes and ask, "Who do you want us to be, Superman?"

The Intersection was actually started as an additional service organized to siphon off 50 people and give us room for more on Sunday mornings. It's working really well, and the siphoning is closer to 100 people, creating lots of open seats for the rest of us to once again fill with our unsaved and hurting friends.

I'm hoping to start churches by gathering together hundreds of our own people and sending them out. We tried that in South Hanover and they all came back, eventually, but the church is doing really well. We sent a couple hundred, and they all came back over time. I've never really succeeded at sending people who stay – usually after the new church is established, they end up coming back. I don't know how to feel about that. But it does make me want to comfort frightened pastors who worry that their entire church will walk out the door never to return, if they dare to plant.

We did succeed at turning South Hanover into a place where new salvations happen, and that's the ultimate goal. Recently, a father and daughter got saved at the South Hanover site, and they still attend there regularly. But sometimes they'll come to our main site because it provides some services and things they can't get at the off-site location. So we work back and forth a lot, especially since all of our sites are within driving distance of one another.

Gap Community Church is another church that I was a small part of planting. I carry that church in my heart, even though they wouldn't necessarily think of us as a parent church. But that's okay.

I met with the pastor, my old friend Merrill Smucker, while he was working through what he wanted to do. He had an aggressive evangelism plan, and I tried to fan the flame of church planting, although he was not open to that at first. I believe it's the best way to bring people into the kingdom, so I just kept planting that seed and then backing off while he prayed about it.

Eventually Merrill came around to the idea of planting a church, and he asked me to stick with him, at least initially, just for mutual mentorship and support. For a while we met weekly involving other pastors, and then we backed off and met monthly, and then more sporadically. When we met, we'd talk about what reaches people, and how excited we get to see lives changed for the better. We shared ideas – his style and mine are radically different, so it was very helpful to me. I picked up five or six huge new ideas that I've implemented at our church, and I hope he picked up a few from me.

I will always carry GCC as a sort of daughter church and a very major deal, even if there was nothing formal there and we were just a very minor partner. But it's so important that we as pastors are willing to do this: help others without getting the credit. Omar's words still bear fruit in my heart: "It's amazing what could get done if we stop worrying about who gets the credit."

I learned this from Omar Beiler in so many ways. In 1994 or 1995 he asked if I would travel with him to the former Soviet Union to meet with pastors there and encourage them. He said that when the wall came down, pastors of churches in Eastern Europe and Asia were mostly untrained – they had never been allowed to receive any kind of formal training under the communist regime – so by the time we got there, they were just dying for encouragement.

Omar arranged for training excursions: pastors from the US would go over there and provide intensive weeks of encouragement and teaching. He was opening up a new missionary field for the Assemblies of God in the country of Armenia. Back then, I didn't even know of a country named Armenia.

"We're going to meet with pastors and find out how to help," he said, "and I think you should come along."

I was very interested in hearing this discussion, so I went.

At one point during our trip, he was sitting there with about thirty pastors, completely untrained, eager to learn, but perhaps a bit skeptical about what we had to offer. They wanted help, but worried about being controlled again - their government had controlled everything about them for decades.

"Listen," he told them, "the Assemblies of God wants to help you. We don't want to control you. We don't want to tell you what to do – we want to partner with you. And by that, I mean we want to be the junior partner. If you will allow us, we will help you and fade. We'll never insist that you give us credit for any of it. You tell us what you need, and we'll do our best to provide, whether it's personnel or training or whatever."

As I listened to him talk about that, the Holy Spirit just leapt inside of my heart. *What could I do in church planting if I took that attitude, if I said, "I don't care who gets the credit or how we do it, just so we get it done?" What if I just took my hands off and said, "Let's catalyze churches?"*

134

At some point during my process of working with Merrill from Gap Community Church, I remember thinking, *I could work like crazy for this and I'll never get credit.* But then I had to ask myself, *Does that really matter?* Ultimately, it can't, and I have to fight down the desire to make everything count for me.

But I will get credit in my own heart. Me and the Holy Spirit will count this — we might be the only ones on earth, but we'll count it because our babies are our babies. And even if they grow up to say they don't want to be our babies, we'll still know their identity. That's okay.

Another church we were involved in was Orchard Springs Church in Bendersville, about ten miles north of Gettysburg. This church originated from a church planter in Carlisle: Tony and Janet DeRosa.

"We're thinking about planting a church. What do you think?"

"That's the most exciting thing I've heard all day. Talk to me."

"Really? You think so?" he asked. "Because most people tell us it's not very exciting."

So we sort of attached ourselves to them at first, especially in prayer. It seemed I was the only encouraging voice they had for a little while. Our mission there was to fan the flame and encourage them. We did end up giving them two portable buildings, worth about $10,000, but we were finished using them and wanted to be team players. We also supported them financially for a couple years.

They do an awesome job reaching people, and we hear about really good fruit coming from them. We're excited about their existence as a church and thank God that it's working and doing well.

Faith, Victory and Life Church was started by a young man in our congregation who came to me and said, "I'm excited about what you said about planting churches. I want to do it."

"Wait a minute," I said. "You're going through a divorce. Your marriage isn't making it – I'm not sure now is the best time to plant a church."

"God told me to do it," he said, cheerfully, "and I'm going to do it whether you help or not. My wife's going to leave me either way."

I think the highest attendance he reached was 15 to 20 people, and eventually they closed.

But listen: there was a victory here, because this young man came back, matured, and is now part of The Intersection site we are starting, with a new humble spirit. Because we were able to maintain a relationship with him through his crisis and his criticism of us. He is a real man of God to this day, and making a real difference in the Kingdom! I love him and do not regret supporting his vision the best we could.

About six years ago, Brian Bolt, a student in our Master's Commission program, pitched his plan to me. It was a plan he learned firsthand from the church that discipled and rescued him from a life of pain and hurtfulness: Victory Churches International. They plant inner city churches around the world. It's the only model for the inner city that I've heard of that works this well. Brian jumped on this model and did it, and it's working. He's already planted his own baby church. Which means I'm a grandpa-church-planter-dude, at least in my head!

This model works, and we're going to plant these churches all around the world.

It's really simple, yet profound. You start with a rehab house that takes addicts off the street and into the pastor's home. For example, if I was the pastor, we'd move into our inner city house and find someone on the street that wants free from something, and we'd tell them to move in with us. The only rehab program they use is discipleship. There are no formal steps or process. There is no curriculum. It's prayer and Bible study and full integration into the life of that church.

We have one now – it's called Freedom House. There are eleven guys in it – it's such a holy gift from God. But we got the idea from Brian.

He had married a girl that he met in our school, the lovely Angelica. Soon both of them moved to Pittsburgh and started inviting men into their home who were hooked on stuff and wanted to be free. They'd lead them to Christ, and these guys would move in with them. They'd fill their home this way and then eventually move out, letting these rehabilitated men take over the rent payments and the house. Then Brian and his wife would get another place. The first guy to "graduate" the program is often the senior leader, sort of in charge of the house.

And that houseful of guys becomes the core of the church. The foundation. The coolest thing is it's such a hot core. They send these guys out to witness to the very drug dealers who used to deal to them, send them back to the neighborhoods they came from. The strategy is not to take these guys out of their situation. It's the exact opposite. The goal is to put them in a position where all their old contacts know about the choice they've made – most of the time, their old friends reject them and won't want them back, but sometimes they are receptive to the gospel. In either case, it's a win-win situation because whatever decision the old friends make, there's now this barrier between the guy and the old lifestyle.

So beautiful.

Every inner city church plant that I ever do will be done that way, until God shows me something better. It's the hardest way, and the best way: hardest because you've got to bare your soul to these guys. You can only communicate Jesus if you know Jesus and hang out with him a lot. So it really puts the pressure on the right places: mainly on the pastor and his wife, to be sure they are living for Jesus in their own home.

Here's how the logistics process went with Brian.

First of all, God arranged a partner for him in Jeff Leak, a great friend from Pittsburgh. He became the primary partner. I didn't have any money – the last church plant had soaked up all our money at that point, and I didn't have any money to give.

What I had was a great young student, ideas and possibilities – I could build connections, and I was catalytic. I can help a guy see how to pull it up out of nothing. That's what I brought to the table in this particular instance.

So I hooked Brian up with a partner and then we (mostly Jeff and his great Allison Park Church) started mapping out a plan. For Brian, that meant starting up a Victory-style church plant based in a recovery home like I described above. We started working that plan, meeting regularly to help and encourage and strengthen. We built a financial plan, which, in Brian's case, came through Jeff Leak's church, (one of Jeff's many strengths).

The process was about a year long, starting with our discussions and decision to get going, all the way through to the first public, regular church service. Brian's church is now about five years old, three or four hundred people, and he has already planted a church and has plans to steadily continue planting. Brian's visibility is unbelievably high – he has a burning passion to know Jesus and to make Jesus known: this is something that cannot be measured.

There is a pain that takes place in birthing a church that I cannot explain to you until you've been through it. I'm not talking about finances (although that part isn't always easy either). Most of the pain I'm talking about comes from this: every young planter starts out identifying themselves by how they're not going to be like the parent-church. It's the same thing a parent goes through when their child grows up.

This becomes so painful for a parent. Most parents end up disconnecting from their kids during this time. Merrill Smucker once explained to me (his kids are older than mine, so he went through this first) that your kids begin to get their identity by seeing how they are different from you. Some of this you have to just sit back and take or you'll end up completely disconnected.

My brother George also helped me during this time. I had asked him if he and his wife Esther would agree to do a weekend of teaching at Freedom Valley, on raising kids well. I admired his kids so much and wanted to raise children as full of Jesus as he had.

George laughed a little with me when I asked him to do it.

"Gerry," he grinned. "Did you ever notice that parents who have already raised their kids don't really want to talk about it anymore? Our kids turned out great by the grace of God, not because we were so good at it. I'm not sure that we have much to give on the subject."

But I pressed him. "Come on, George", I insisted. "You are my big brother and you can't get away with this as easy as that. If you won't do the teaching, at least give me something!"

"Okay," he finally relented. "One really big part of being a parent is just standing there and taking it."

"What?" I asked. "But what about discipline and respect? And nurture and training, and... well, so many other things?"

"Well, kids naturally criticize their parents. And that's not all bad. It's just how they develop their identity. If you can let them do this without freaking out or feeling like they're disrespecting you, if you can get through this process, then you can be friends afterward. Because when they are finished talking about the things about you they don't want to be, then they start talking about the things that they do want to copy. And that's a great time, a fun process. But if you get completely disconnected during the difficult stage you'll miss out on it."

The same thing happens in church planting.

A young person comes to me and says, "I want to plant a church, and it's not going to be a stupid one like Freedom Valley, it's going to be relevant. I don't want to do anything like you guys do it."

If I can hold my tongue during this time and maintain my composure at that point, then I can keep the discussion going and the relationship intact.

"I know we do some things really bad," I try to say, "and even I wouldn't do a lot of things like us. Tell me how you are going to be different."

This starts them on a process where they begin to tear you down, but hang in there.

"The worship needs to change, and the sermons aren't memorable enough" and on and on and on. It's so painful. But I know that if I can keep my composure through that discussion, and the many difficult discussions that will come in those early days, good things will happen.

You know what? It isn't long after they've planted their church that they come back to me, singing a different tune.

"How do you guys do that so well?" they'll ask, shaking their heads in amazement. They'll go on, too, listing the things they're struggling with, asking for ideas on how to improve. But they never would have come back for this if I would have torn them down early in the process, when they sounded critical.

Nobody said following Jesus would be easy, He certainly didn't. But if we work with Him to build His church, there is a sense of destiny, and an amazing value to be gained for our world.

Chapter Thirteen: Rejection Triage

"But if a town refuses to welcome you..."

People seem to have a lot of odd ideas about what it means to be a pastor. One guy asked me if we "sit around and pray all day." Others think it must be the easiest job in the world because, in their minds, it basically involves nice, kind people, thinking warm thoughts about God, and a lot of singing.

I don't entirely blame them. As I look back over 27 years of ministry, I often wonder if any of my thoughts about what it was really like were accurate. My two main mentors adjusted every thought I had about being a pastor. I just did not have a functional thought about serving in the ministry, or how church should look.

One seasoned leader told me that his biggest struggle with being a pastor was the burden of people's secrets.

"Sooner or later, you hear about every bad moment, every regrettable incident, and every painful consequence a person can suffer. The junk of the entire community ends up in your ears," he said, "and sometimes you wonder if there are any healthy people anywhere. Then you look in the mirror and the truth of the human condition becomes inescapable."

He's not wrong. And these issues are why the Bible was written, why Jesus died, and why we get a timeless explanation of how it got this way. But we're also given hope that we can get out of the mess.

Yet the largest pain of leadership has to be rejection.

Jesus tried to prepare his disciples for the rejection they would face, but I never felt completely prepared. God saw fit to give me a gift of mercy, which gave me a very tender heart. As such, I was someone who felt rejection very young.

I remember, perhaps at five or six years old, my father planned an adventure with my four older brothers. One of them had asked him innocently enough where the local railroad tracks went. Dad loves trains and everything about them. He replied by telling him that one day they would walk those tracks and discover for themselves where they went.

I was so excited on the chosen day. I got up early and laced up my little shoes, which was no small achievement for a little guy my size. As my big brothers prepared to leave, I made sure I was ready and good to go in every way I could be.

My dad, however, saw my eager face and took me aside.

"You will never be able to keep up," he told me, "and we will not be able to carry you all those miles. I'm sorry, but you can't go with us today. When you get older, maybe I'll take you on one of these little adventures. But not today."

My little heart felt so crushed. So rejected. I wept for hours. My dad and I never did get to walk those train tracks together. I was learning even at a young age that life had a lot of rejection in it.

Later, when I was 27 or 28 years old and had been in ministry for a while as our church's youth pastor. Our senior pastor Omar came to me and made clear his intention to enter the mission field.

"When I leave, I'd like you to consider taking over as lead pastor here," he said.

I was honored but also felt slightly confused.

"I just don't know, Omar. I really feel called to plant a new church, not take over this one – besides, I don't think this church would ever accept me." I thought my age would be a problem for some of the folks in our church.

"Why don't you just think about it?" he asked.

"Okay, I'll think about it."

Six months later I got back to him.

"I've prayed about it, and I'll do it."

So he put my name in at one of the board meetings, nominating me to take over as senior pastor.

Not too much later, the board not only voted down my nomination, but they asked me to leave. Or go plant a church. At least 50 miles away, one member said, so you don't confuse this church body.

I felt like I had gotten fired.

Omar kept saying, "We're promoting you to your dream! Your dream was to plant a church, and that's what we're encouraging you to do!"

"But you had asked me to take on your dream, and then the board basically asked me to go away. Can you blame me for feeling fired?"

I was so hurt and felt that my own church had rejected me. I felt like a man without a country. Pastors have somewhat of a unique role in a community, where their job, church, and friendships are often all balled up into one entity. When parishioners lose a job, they still have their church and their friends, but if a pastor loses their job, they usually lose everything at once.

I was doing some work for a local computer company, and at one point the client came in, someone I knew, and asked me how I was doing.

Simple question, right?

I started answering her, but then I just lost it. I completely broke down. This was the fragile state that the entire situation had put me in: I blubbered like a kid. The client tried to stand there and comfort me, but I finally just walked out the door and got in my car and drove home. I laid in my bed and bawled my eyes out.

"God," I said. "If this is the way you treat ministers, then I'm not in anymore. I'm out."

So I called my presbyter, the guy over me in the Assemblies of God, Elmer Kipe.

"Elmer, I'm in over my head. I need help. I'm not functioning. It's been six months since I've been left go from my old church. I'm supposed to be planting a church but I can't do anything. Will you meet with me?"

"Sure, I'll buy you lunch. Meet me wherever you'd like."

So a few days later I met with him.

"Elmer," I said, "can you believe I got fired?"

"Well, you didn't really get fired," he said. "You got approved to plant a church and that was your vision."

"I know, but I was asked to go away. Now my friends don't know how to talk to me. I don't have any income. I don't know what to do with myself. And I didn't think I would ever move out of this area, but now I feel like I have to. My wife is crying. I'm crying all the time. I just can't function."

Elmer just looked at me, and he got really quiet for a while. I thought I must have stumped him. What he finally said could have knocked me over.

"Gerry, I'm in my fifties. I'm here to tell you that I don't know any pastors that haven't gone through this."

"What?" I exclaimed.

"I don't know any pastors that haven't gone through this," he repeated. "Let me ask you a question: Who did you think you were following?"

Hurt and angry, I responded with arrogance.

"I'm following Jesus – who are you following?"

"What did they do to Jesus?" he asked, kindly ignoring my attitude.

"Elmer, I think Jesus died on the cross as a substitution for me, you know, so I wouldn't have to go through that."

"That's not what the Bible says. I don't know where you got that idea, but I think you got it from the enemy of your soul, not the lover of your soul."

"What are you talking about?"

Elmer rocked my world as I wept in that booth in the back of a restaurant.

"Jesus said that if you don't take up your cross and follow him, you're not worthy of him. Gerry, I just have to ask you, do you want to follow Jesus or not? You don't have to. There are other ways to live. I don't blame you if you don't want to. But this is what it's like. It's going to hurt. It's going to cost you."

I stared at him, and he continued.

"You need to get a picture of what this whole mess is worth, and what good this will do in your life. In Luke 10 Jesus said I'm sending you out like a lamb among wolves. Gerry, do you get that? You are the lamb. One of these is the eater, and the other is the eatee, and you are the eatee. In other words, Jesus is sending you out to be ripped up."

Once again we sat there in silence. His words were seeping into my innermost being.

"I don't blame you if you don't want to be in the ministry," he continued. "I don't always want to be in the ministry. But I'm telling you, this is what it is, and this is what following Jesus is going to be like sometimes."

In those days we were in the middle of a huge positive thinking wave, and our society was permeated by Norman Vincent Peale's "The Power of a Positive Mind." Omar and I were really into that stuff. I needed it, don't get me wrong. I was a negative thinker. But all of that positive thinking had me convinced that bad stuff didn't have to happen, that hard times didn't have to come along.

"I don't know how this fits in with all this positive thinking material," Elmer continued, "but Jesus said I am sending you out as a lamb among wolves. That is a bloody, painful mess. Every day. If you don't want to follow Jesus, no problem, do what you want to do. But follow Jesus, and this is how it's going to be for the rest of your life."

145

I just kept crying. I put my head down on my arms.

"I don't think I can do this," I said, barely able to talk.

I have to be honest: I have never wanted to punch someone in the mouth with my full force more than I wanted to hit Elmer that day. I wanted to pound him into the ground, because he was telling me the pain I was in was something I needed to be prepared to take for the rest of my life. Why?

Because this process clarifies vision. Vision is only worth living for when you would rather die than not have it.

Ironically, that's when life gets fun.

I spoke with Omar recently.

"You're doing ministry in the 10/40 window," I told him. "That's where people die!"

"Gerry, the more I talk about how dangerous it is to preach Jesus in a Muslim culture, the more people sign up. It's ridiculous. It shouldn't work this way, but it does. When I talk in my missions services about how signing up for this might lead to you never coming back, I get at least three couples raising their hands, asking when they can go."

"What is wrong with that picture?" I asked, shaking my head in disbelief.

"Nothing at all," he said. "People want something worth dying for. If you don't give people something worth dying for, you're not giving them something worth living for, either."

An old friend of mine from Bible college is now a missionary in the most Muslim nation on earth. I could tell you his name, but it would endanger him. One of the first times I had him to our church to speak, I asked him a question.

"How do you handle the fact that, when you leave your house in the morning, you're not sure whether or not you'll come back that day? You have three little children! How do you face your kids with that – 'I don't know if I'm coming back today, but God bless you.'"

He just smiled and answered my question with a question.

"Gerry, what does a kid want more than anything from their father?"

"I guess that their father would be their hero," I said, already understanding. "Not very many kids have that these days. A lot of kids hate their dads, or don't even have dads."

"Every boy hungers to think of their dad as their hero," he confirmed, "and they'll hang on to that way beyond when it's even possible. There's something in a kid that desperately wants that. If you get up at a funeral and don't say something nice about a kid's dad, that kid would hate you for the rest of your life."

"The message I give my children when I walk out the door each morning," he continued, "is that if I don't come back today, I lived a life worth dying for. How many kids can say that about their dad? If I get killed today, and my daughter is three years old, I've given my daughter something that most fathers never give their kids."

"Wow," I said.

"Gerry, I pray frequently, 'God, if I can, I would like to die a martyr for what I believe in. If I can! Is there any way you can work that out for me?'"

I sat there and something came alive in me that had never been alive before. Our kids are about the same age, and I knew what it was like to have little ones looking me in the eye.

Was I being a hero for them?

I walked out of that meeting with Elmer completely crushed. But when God put my vision back together, I finally knew what I wanted so well that I could taste it. I didn't care if Omar laughed at me, or Merrill, or my wife, or the board, or my parents.

Everybody has to reach that point. If Omar hadn't laughed at me when I was a young man wanting to preach, if the board at our church hadn't pushed me away, if that pastor in Gettysburg hadn't mocked my vision...I bet if none of those things had happened, I may not even be able to remember my original calling.

147

But each of these wolves, in attacking my vision, only ingrained it deeper and deeper into my psyche. If more pastors would mock me even more, then I would probably be even stronger!

God is still calling out to people who are willing to take up their cross and follow Jesus. The cross you are asked to take up, dear reader, is the instrument of your own death. I don't blame you if you choose not to follow this Jesus or live this life. If you choose it, it will be hard and it will cost you. It will be worth it all in the end. But it will cost you.

The choice is all yours.

Chapter Fourteen: Party Carefully

"When the 72 disciples returned, they joyfully reported to him, 'Lord, even the demons obey us when we use your name!'"

So the 70 disciples come back to Jesus after he sent them out. They healed the sick and told everyone that the kingdom of heaven is near them. Then they come back. He never told them to come back, but they do, and when they do, they are rejoicing!

"Even devils submit to us in your name!" they shout.

They were so high on this new authority they had, this new skill of casting out devils. They were so pumped about making a difference. But Jesus stops them.

I struggled with this a little while ago. Why wouldn't he high-five them and jump around with them? Why wouldn't he pat their backs and smile and take them down to a seaside party?

Jesus understands that they have a new found power, but he says, "don't rejoice just because evil spirits obey you. Rejoice because your names are registered as citizens of heaven." Why, instead of celebrating with them, does he issue this reminder?

God resists the proud. The only thing that can stop a believer is pride. There's no devil that can stop us. We have the authority in Jesus name and we have triumphed over the devil in Jesus' name. The devil can't stop us.

But we can stop ourselves.

The way we stop ourselves is by becoming proud. Arrogance will put up a barrier, fast. So when the disciples came back, celebrating this power, Jesus told them they should be celebrating more about the fact that their names are registered as citizens of heaven.

Celebrating your newfound skills will always lead to pride. I think this affects churches because many of us think we have got the one and only program that works. We think we are at the cutting edge, and we're getting it done. Yet this type of thinking will destroy us.

As pastors, we have to teach this to our people. Don't celebrate your church, or your church will be destroyed. Celebrate instead how God reached down and, in his grace, chose us even though we still don't deserve it. This is what we should celebrate, because this is what keeps us humble.

I'm trying to get our Freedom Valley folks (especially their pastor) to stop talking like this:

"I know you went to that church but THIS is the best church in the county – you ought to come here because we are the best place around."

This leads to people giving up on church. How?

Well, if they're attending the best church in the world, and it lets them down, then what? They stop going to church, because they just had the best and it failed them. But what if they don't have the mindset that Freedom Valley is the only church out there worth going to? If they get hurt and leave, then maybe they'll at least be open to looking for another place.

If I do what Paul says, and I consider others better than myself, I'll say something to new believers that sounds more like this:

"You know what? We are so glad you are here. But Bethel Assembly of God is a better church – if you want a better church, go there. Over here is First Baptist, and in New Oxford is the United Methodist Church: all better churches than ours. We're okay. We're doing our best. God called us for one thing, and we're doing our best to do that."

Talking like this gives you credibility with new people. And it is true to the spirit of The Kingdom, where we all think of others as better than ourselves.

Then the first time someone gets hurt by someone in your church (and everybody, everybody, everybody gets hurt in church) they'll say, "I don't need this church. There are better ones out there." And they'll go to this other church. Very possibly they'll connect, but at least they're staying in the kingdom. But more than likely they'll come back and say, "Yeah, that church is better but this is the one I'm called to." Many of these folks will have a stronger commitment in the long run.

I think our number one problem in America is that we are so fond of saying, "My church is the best church." That's why I keep telling my people the same message.

"You know," I'll say, "Scripture says we ought to consider others better than ourselves. So I think Bethel Assembly is probably a better church than Freedom Valley."

Sometimes, after hearing me teach this, my people will come up to me after the church with a question.

"Why do you have such bad self-esteem?"

Commonly in our culture, if you believe someone else is better than you, that's seen as poor self-esteem. But it's not! It's the opposite! Because I'm strong enough and believe in myself enough to like you better than I like me. That is a strength, not a weakness.

Believing your church is the best is not healthy for long-term, kingdom strategy. If your strategy is to grow the biggest church in the next five years then, great, talk up your church and put down other churches. Say, "don't go there, come here, we're better." But that's not Christ, and it's not a strategy that will benefit the kingdom long-term.

When Jesus conveyed this idea of partying carefully, he was trying to stop us from focusing on how great we think our theology, programs or church is. None of those things will create strong believers. Celebrate other people's greatness. Celebrate that your name is written in the Lamb's book of life.

One way that we at Freedom Valley work on this concept is by keeping a brochure in the foyer entitled "Other Great Churches You Ought To Try in Adams County." I like having this available for numerous reasons.

First, when new believers come to me and say things like, "I love this church, because this is where I decided to follow Jesus, but why don't you ever do hymns? I haven't been in church for 20 years, but that's what I remember."

"You know what," I say, "there are so many other great churches that sing hymns in Adams County."

"Where?"

"I'll make you a list of other churches you should try," I said. "They're all better than us, and they all sing hymns."

So I started publishing this list, and we replenish it at the rate of 100-200 copies each month. There's a little map in there and everything.

If we have a kingdom mindset, it really doesn't matter where someone goes to church. If the 168 people who got saved at our church at Harvest Cry this year all end up going to other churches, there would be nothing wrong with that.

After we built our building in the year 2000, we went through a three-year, absurdly high growth surge. We jumped to an attendance of 1800 pretty quick, then dipped back down to 1100 and stayed there for a few years. It drove me crazy.

Now that I look back, though, I think there is an explanation: the bottom line is, we were pretty proud.

We talked humble, we hoped we were humble, but we weren't. We were arrogant. That's what I think. We celebrated the wrong things: our new buildings, our newfound popularity, the fact that everyone knew our name and who we were. I should have, during those times, pulled my staff together and emphasized that we should never talk about how great our church is, or what a wonderful job we were doing.

We should have been coaching our new believers along these lines, but we didn't. So most of the folks who joined our church in those days still think Freedom Valley is the best thing since sliced bread, and it's taking us some time to change that mindset. To turn that whole ship around, when the ship was based on the idea that we had it all together and were the experts in the county on church, is a difficult undertaking.

We rapidly lost momentum because we got proud and partied over the wrong things.

Chapter Fifteen: The Plan

When the religious people of Jesus' time complained that he was spending too much time with what they considered the losers and the rabble of society, Jesus told a parable about a shepherd who lost one sheep:

Tax collectors and other notorious sinners often came to listen to Jesus teach. This made the Pharisees and teachers of religious law complain that he was associating with such despicable people – even eating with them! So Jesus used this illustration: if you had 100 sheep, and one strayed away and was lost in the wilderness, would you leave the 99 others to go and search for the lost one until you found it? And then you would joyfully carry it home on your shoulders. (Luke 15: 1-9)

The wonderful heart of God breaks over the loss of one solitary sheep. Just one. But if the numbers for the Northeast hold true across the country, 83% of people in our country are lost sheep. That's not just one sheep out of a hundred – that's 83 lost sheep. What job review would be given to a shepherd who lost 83 of his 100 sheep?

Wouldn't you leave 17 sheep in order to recover 83?

During the last 25 years I have grappled with these questions again and again. Where are they all going? Why have they left? What can we do to bring them back? I am not content to sit back and watch while more and more people in this country walk away from Christ and the kingdom life that he makes available.

You can't say people haven't tried. In fact, we've tried all kinds of things, and they all worked in their own way and their own time, but so far nothing has been done to stem the tide of people leaving the church in our culture.

Billy Graham crusades were great. God give us more evangelists like him, with the effectiveness and character that he is known for. But even with all of those commitments to Christ, churches are still emptying.

Years ago there was a plan to distribute the gospel of Mark on video to every home in America. One was delivered to my house. Our youngest son Luke watched it at four years old, and we found him kneeling on the floor in front of the TV, committing his life to Jesus. We rejoiced with him, and even as a very small church helped distribute hundreds of them to many homes in our community.

But in the 15 years or so since that video was released, sheep continue to leave the flock.

Before that, we tried door-to-door evangelism, sending out teams to reach their neighbors and pass out tracts. We bought them by the case, and distributed them to everyone we could find. Then there was Christian television, and Christian radio. And so many other ideas and plans.

Yet the number of people who attend our existing churches continues to diminish.

What will make the difference in our time?

I believe that the best answer is what Paul did in Acts. He traveled everywhere, evangelizing and transforming the known world by planting churches. He didn't have to. He could have stayed in Jerusalem and tried to build a mega church. He could have stayed in Israel and ensured that the original church was healthy or financially stable before heading out.

But he didn't. He left. He hit the road. Why?

Because new churches attract new people. New churches provide the new wine skins that Jesus spoke of. New churches try new things to get the gospel to people who have otherwise never heard a presentation of the gospel that makes sense to them.

Churches in North America are on birth control. Rarely will a church give birth to another church. But if we got serious about reaching our world, it would require as many as half of all churches to get involved in planting churches. If we did this, within the next 100 years, we could seriously change the momentum and begin to reach American culture.

It's been done before. It can be done again.

Toward the end of the 19th century, as America fought in the Civil War, Christians got a vision of what could be. The United States Christian Commission for example, created robust and effective ministries to reach soldiers and bring them into eternal life. Even in the Gettysburg battles that happened a few miles from where I am writing, thousands of soldiers attended evangelistic services at night, coming to Christ perhaps the night before they died in battle. Some 50,000 casualties were reported in the three days of battle here in Gettysburg alone.

In the years after the Civil War, churches in America began aggressively planting new churches. They gained on the culture, seeing a majority of Americans come to Christ and commit themselves to a local body of believers.

Less than 50 years after the Civil War, some denominations and Christian groups started talking about running out of people to reach! The majority of Americans were attending church, and the blessing of God was upon us again. By the 1930s, some denominations were suggesting that we should slow down the church planting machines, because we were getting the job done.

Several decades later, the effort to slow down church planting, was working. By the 1950s and 60s, we had no increase in the number of churches being started, and Christianity in America was growing no longer.

I started ministry in the early 80s, hoping that somehow we could once again see America move toward God. We tried every evangelistic and outreach method that we could find. To this day we go after any event, outreach plan, or cultural system that will help us lead one more person to Christ.

Perhaps the one that could make all the difference is the one that worked before: planting churches! It worked in Acts. It worked in post Civil War America. It could work again today.

A few years ago, I started working with Johannes Amritzer, an evangelist from Sweden. In early 2010 I traveled with him to Nepal where we conducted a crusade in the city of Butwal. Dozens of churches worked together diligently to reach their city, and we supported them.

By the time we left Nepal, all 2000 salvation booklets that we had taken with us were given out to new believers in response to altar calls. The churches began working together to welcome in these new believers and to start new churches to reach their city.

That's when jealousy hit me: I want that for my city.

For my nation.

What if five or ten churches in a given city banded together to hold a similar campaign and reach their area? What if the result was thousands of new believers, each of whom could be shepherded into new communities of faith?

What if this started happening all over America, until we saw our cities ablaze with salvation, forgiveness, restoration, healing, and all kinds of signs and wonders? What's keeping us from doing this?

I tried to do this once and money wasn't the issue, as long as I could get ten to twelve churches involved. The location was available, and the people in our city were interested. But it still didn't happen. Why?

The thing that kept this from moving forward was the fear of local churches that new churches would take their people and put them out of business. Just when we were getting close to making it happen, pastors started getting worried. I understand this fear – you can't run a church without people and the resources they bring to the table. But we as pastors have to embrace the fear and realize that planting churches will not lead to our church diminishing in any way – it will actually lead to an explosion of growth!

When will your church get off of birth control?

When will your church start producing baby churches?

You can do it. We can all do it. And we have to, if we want to see sheep returning to the shepherd.

The Harvest is ready.

What do you see?

Epilogue:
A Letter From One Lost Sheep, Now Found

Dear Gerry,

As you may or may not know, I was brought up in a very negative, critical, and abusive environment. Words of true kindness and encouragement were not spoken over me (as a matter of fact, it was the exact opposite), and goals and dreams were anything but encouraged. To say the very least, my home life was not an ideal situation.

But I don't blame my parents because that's all they knew. They were brought up in very similar households. And my mom did the best she could as a divorced parent with the little we had to raise me and my three sisters. When I initially, and very reluctantly, expressed my desire with her to go to Nepal, her reply was exactly what I expected (based on previous experience), but it was still very difficult to hear and hard to accept.

"You'll never be able to do it," were the exact words that came out of her mouth.

How unbelievably crushing! Parents, in my opinion, should be nurturing and encouraging. They should challenge their children to dream and gently nudge them towards their goals and visions, but that was not the environment that my sisters and I were brought up in.

159

My mom was basically paralyzed with fear from years of verbal and physical abuse, and nothing but perfection was acceptable in my father's eyes. So, I basically grew up feeling afraid to hope or dream or have aspirations. And, even if one dared to scale my towering wall of fear, I learned very early on how to squelch it; it was much safer not to try than to do so and risk imperfection or even worse: complete failure (or so I was taught).

But that all changed when I crossed the threshold to Freedom Valley!

To this day, I thank God that you prayed "curiosity" over the property because it's definitely one of things that drew me there. I can remember driving by and wondering why so many people were there at all hours of the day and night (day in & day out). I wondered what they were doing and what made them want to be there so often. I wondered why there were horses outside and a riding arena. I wondered why the building looked like, in my opinion, a large shed, and why there was no steeple. I wondered why there was a neon "Open" sign in the window and why it was called a worship center as opposed to a church.

I still don't have answers to all of my questions, but I'm totally ok with that! Figuring them out will, hopefully, keep me around for awhile!

And to this day, I am so grateful for the wonderful, amazing people that I have grown to know and love there! As I've shared before, I've never met or been part of a group that has made me feel so accepted and loved (flaws and all).

Day after day, week after week, month after month, I continue to be greeted and welcomed by the warmest smiles, life-changing words of encouragement, and the most awesome, rib-and-spine-crushing hugs in all of Adams County (and, more than likely, well beyond!) I am so very honored to call you my pastor and to be a member of Freedom Valley. I am so very blessed to call it my home!

Millie

ACKNOWLEDGMENTS

For the past ten years or more, Brian Sauder has asked me to share our church planting story in the Dove Leadership School. Two years ago, he asked me if I had ever considered writing this book. I had often thought about it, but I needed the push that his suggestions and encouragement provided.

I am a bit of a flower-child dreamer, given to big visions but little motivation to make them happen. If God had not put Marvin Stanley in my life to help me get some of these crazy ideas done, I don't think many of them would have ever happened. Marvin takes my ideas, helps me identify the obstacles, then systematically and unwaveringly dismantles whatever mountains threaten our forward progress. He and Jason Fitch are men of unbelievable courage, patience, and kindness to me.

Lorrie, my administrative assistant, and her husband Wayne, are one amazing, patient couple. Every step is productive and every word encouraging. I cannot even imagine my life without their friendship. Of the many, many things Mark and Connie Keller have done to make Freedom Valley so productive, bringing Wayne and Lorrie into it had to be one of the best! To this day when the Kellers and Reddings get behind something, demons come out with their hands up.

Over the past few years, Luke, our youngest son, relentlessly encouraged me to write this book. His desire to read it and tell his friends about it brought me so much inspiration. Evan debated concepts and discussed ideas with me and kept the fire burning. Shawna inspired me with her own writing skills, far surpassing mine, but giving me courage to try nonetheless. Her initial feedback to the first draft fueled my brain with so much creativity. Candace joined my team recently by volunteering to do the one job nobody else wanted, and doing it so well that lots of people stand in line for it now. I love her even more for that.

I love and admire my kids so much.

Thank you to all of my volunteer editors: Janice Phipps, Julie Stoltzfoos, Charity Landis, Janice Riley, Shawna Lewis, Sandra

Cullison, Cathy Gross, Pam Olshanski, Elizabeth Monfort, Merrill Smucker, Ryan Dagen and so many others! You guys made it great!

Shawn Smucker, my co-writer, made this project possible, kept it on track, and made it fun to read. Shawn, you are an amazing gift!

I owe so much to the first eight site pastors who totally bought into the vision and now lead me as much as I lead them: Jeff Miller, Jason Fitch, Jeremiah Herbert, Rick Roth, Jeff Deitrich, Rob Costello, and Rich Fogal. We are men of more passion than wisdom, and more refusal to give up than great plans, but I'd rather go to battle with you guys than anybody I know. Remember, "the least of you will be a thousand!" Thanks for letting me be on your teams!

Freedom Valley, I still wonder why you show up to hear me preach. Thank you for being the vision-filled, powerful people who never give up, never walk away, and never stop believing that the same God who started this good work in us will complete it! Most of you are first generation Christians, but your amazing faith and unrelenting desire to get one more person in the door to Jesus will change the world forever! I love you and am so proud to know you!

Thank you for allowing me the great privilege of being your Pastor.

SOURCES

1. Dr. Ronnie W. Floyd. "Progress Report of the Great Commission Resurgence Task Force of the Southern Baptist Convention," pg 9

2. http://www.edstetzer.com/2010/03/march-outreach-church-birth-co.html

ABOUT THE AUTHORS

Gerry Stoltzfoos is the lead pastor at Freedom Valley Worship Center, York Road Site in Gettysburg, Pennsylvania, where he lives with his wife Julie. His original vision, "to reach those who have given up on church," is still their central focus.

Gerry blogs at http://gerrystoltzfoos.blogspot.com and can be reached at gerry@freedomvalley.org

Shawn Smucker lives in Paradise, Pennsylvania with his wife Maile and their four children. He has co-written two other books: *Think No Evil* (the story of how the Amish impacted the world with their message of forgiveness after the Nickel Mines school shooting), and *Twist of Faith* (the story of Auntie Anne's Soft Pretzels founder, Anne Beiler).

Shawn blogs at http://shawnsmucker.com and can be reached at shawnsmucker@yahoo.com